TODDLERS AND THEIR MOTHERS

Abridged Version

for Parents and Educators

Toddlers and Their Mothers

Abridged Version for Parents and Educators

Erna Furman

INTERNATIONAL UNIVERSITIES PRESS, INC.
MADISON, CONNECTICUT

Second Printing, 1994

Library of Congress Cataloging-in-Publication Data

Furman, Erna.
    Toddlers and their mothers: abridged version for parents and
educators/Erna Furman.
        p.   cm.
    Includes bibliographical references and index.
    ISBN 0-8236-8318-4
    1. Personality development. 2. Mother and child. 3. Child
analysis. I. Title.
BF723.P4F87 1993
155.42'382—dc20   93-1871
                                                                                     CIP

Manufactured in the United States of America

Contents

Preface

As soon as the original *Toddlers and Their Mothers* was published, both professionals and parents urged me to write a second version, one for parents and educators. None of the text is watered down, but only those topics were included here which would be of special interest to the readers who live with, and care for and about, toddlers.

Erna Furman

Acknowledgments

This study was helped by many people in many ways. My appreciation and gratitude extend to all of them. First and foremost, I wish to thank the toddlers and their families who have worked with us, and the child analysts and educators who participated directly in the joint endeavor. Of the fifteen child analysts who have thus far carried out treatment-via-the-parent, analyses, and contributed all along by sharing their observations and understanding, the following have, in addition, devoted much time, thought, and effort to reviewing the successive metapsychological profiles of their cases: Thomas F. Barrett, Ph.D., Elizabeth Daunton, Ruth Hall, Jean Kushleika, Amy Lipkowitz, Joanne Naegele, Barbara Streeter, Carl Tuss, and Lorraine Weisman. Phyllis Wapnick, the Toddler Group teacher, and Ginny Steininger, the Hanna Perkins educational director, have worked with me untiringly in implementing the educational program and coordinating it with our nursery school and its staff. I am especially grateful to Dr. Thomas F. Barrett, who, as associate director of the toddler research, spent countless hours in sharing the arduous task of constructing the toddler profile outline, of working out and reviewing the individual profiles, and of discussing the implications of the assembled data.

I am deeply appreciative of the enthusiastic support of the Hanna Perkins Board of Trustees for the toddler program and of the Cleveland Foundation's generous financial contribution to the work of the toddler research project.

For this, the Abridged Version, I am especially grateful to Penelope Leach who persuaded me to write it, and whose many books, such as *Your Baby and Child* (1989), have been many parents' valuable companions during their children's infancy.

Last but not least, I thank my husband, Robert A. Furman, M.D., whose dedicated and effective efforts and contributions to all aspects of this work have been so essential and invaluable, from setting up and administering the toddler group, right down to reading and critiquing the manuscript, always with a kind but steady hand at the helm.

Erna Furman

PART I.

How We Work

CHAPTER 1

The Hanna Perkins
Mother–Toddler Group

THE SETTING

This book describes some of our experiences with the Hanna Perkins Mother–Toddler Group. Just as specific observations of a child become meaningful only in the context of his overall personality functioning and life experiences, so the observations and findings of a study have to be understood within the framework in which all the participants contribute to the shared experience. I shall therefore begin by describing the setting, at least briefly, and refer the interested reader to the more detailed and extensive account given in the unabridged edition of *Toddlers and Their Mothers* (E. Furman, 1992).

The Hanna Perkins School was founded in 1950 to provide education and treatment for young children with emotional disturbances. Closely linked with its twin agency, the Cleveland Center for Research in Child Development, it has maintained a nursery school and kindergarten with sixteen children in each (R. A. Furman and A. Katan, 1969). Operating as nonprofit private agencies with a liberal sliding fee scale, the School and Center have served families with varied socioeconomic, ethnic, racial, and religious backgrounds. Using psychoanalytic principles, education and therapy have always been dovetailed, and

3

parents have actively participated in the teamwork with teachers and child psychoanalysts. With the children's problems ranging from minor developmental conflicts to major pathologies, the therapeutic interventions have been weekly treatment-via-the-parent, a method especially developed at our school (E. Furman, 1957, 1969a, 1980), or individual analysis of the child, with the parents seen weekly as well by the child's analyst. While the therapy helps parents and child understand and resolve individual problems, it relies on and utilizes the teachers' skilled observations of the child's functioning in the school setting, and their provision of an educational milieu that fosters healthy development and constructive use of newly freed energy.

Our work with toddlers initially focused on the younger siblings of the preschoolers who attended our nursery and kindergarten. The parents' concerns with the upbringing of these infants and toddlers were always part of the work with the therapist, and we often got to know the little ones well when they accompanied mother to therapy sessions and to bring and pick up the older children at school. Then, some twenty years ago, the Center, through its Extension Service, initiated a course "Working with Toddlers." Today it continues to provide consultation and assistance to groups of directors and caregivers from many different centers with toddler or mother–toddler groups in the area. It is one of the ways in which we share our findings and learn from the experiences of others.

Finally, in 1985 we established our own Mother–Toddler Group. It enrolls six toddlers, 18 months to 3 years old, each accompanied and cared for by his or her mother or mothering person. Depending on age and development, the children attend for one to two years, twice weekly from 9:30 to 11 A.M. The majority then progresses to our Nursery School. As with all Hanna Perkins children, these toddlers are "at risk," with difficulties ranging from minor developmental conflicts to major disturbances in personality growth. However, comparison with numerous nontherapeutic centers shows that our toddlers' troubles are no greater, and often smaller, than those in the "normal" groups. What distinguishes our toddlers is their parents. They care about their child so much and in such a way that they have overcome the special hurt of recognizing that a child has a difficulty and of being willing to work on it. To that end, they are prepared to commit themselves to a therapeutic-educational undertaking which involves considerable practical and emotional burdens over a long period. This parental investment and effort are their prerequisite strength, regardless of their personal troubles or interferences in their relationships with their child. They may master or mitigate these difficulties sufficiently through the work, or they may seek separate therapeutic help for themselves while continuing to work with the child analyst and teachers on behalf of their child.

There are special prerequisites for the staff too. Among a number of compelling reasons for establishing the Toddler Program there is a personal one: I like toddlers. Professionals, like mothers, have individual preferences for different developmental phases. Excellent nursery school teachers may be uncomfortable with toddlers; excellent caregivers for toddlers may not make good preschool educators. The toddler phase, with its primitive vulnerable self and strong "uncivilized" impulses, poses special threats to the adult personality. It also makes special demands, even such mundane ones as having to become multilingual because each toddler speaks his own verbal and nonverbal language. Yet, for those who enjoy being with toddlers, feeling with, and understanding them, there are special satisfactions, among them to enter, or reenter, a world in which maternal functioning still constitutes an integral part of the child's personality, and to assist the mother–child couple in negotiating this crucial phase. Just as the mother's support, encouragement, and containment is necessary for the toddler to function and grow, so the helping professionals need to feel with the mother–toddler couple, understand the mutual intricacies of their relationship, and extend themselves in an encompassing way to assist them with mastery. This role is similar to the one the father fulfills with mother and toddler in the family (R. A. Furman, 1983; E. Furman, 1987). The professional, however, has to understand and support the father in his role as well, and must not become either the "better" mother or father by taking over their parts, but instead appreciate and aid in the delicate balance of their interactions.

To accomplish this difficult emotional task, the professionals, in turn, need full support for their work with the toddlers and their families, and this support has to come from the setting in which the work takes place. Just as in the family the toddler has to be a welcome member, provided for, appreciated, cared about, respected, and given space (in every sense of the word), so those who work with toddlers need to be able to rely on and benefit from the caring interest and practical help of everyone in their agency, from cook to director, from receptionist to the Board of Trustees. Each person makes his important contribution, each, as in a big family, makes sacrifices and takes on some extra work because they invest themselves in the toddler work, rejoice in its progress, share in and try to mitigate its hardships. Experience with many agencies has shown that this dedicated, unconditional support is crucial to the success of toddler work and care. The Hanna Perkins Mother–Toddler Group has been very fortunate in being welcomed with broad-based understanding and in being able to count on each and everyone's full support. Unlike the toddler in the family, who has the right to take this for granted, we who work with the Toddler Group are deeply appreciative and recognize it as an indispensable part of our work.

PREPARING FOR ENTRY TO TODDLER GROUP

Most parents have completed the intake procedure during spring or summer and begun to work with the child analyst assigned to them before the start of the school year. About a week prior to the first day of class, we invite them to an open house, where they meet with the teachers, get acquainted with the setting, learn about our educational program, and get help in preparing their child. On the first day of school, they arrive at our adjacent parking lot or walk from the nearby bus stop, are greeted by the receptionist, and proceed down the hallway. The Toddler Group is timed to assure that the hallway is clear of the older children's comings and goings. The toddler room is located between the nursery and kindergarten rooms, but isolated from them by a storage room on each side. It is about

25 by 25 feet in size. Next to the door are the children's cubbies for their clothes and belongings (mothers' coats are hung in a hall closet). Each child's cubby is marked with an individual color and his or her name, and there is one bathroom, with a toilet and sink. When in use, the bathroom door is closed to ensure privacy. A second, also private bathroom is available in the hallway, near the toddler room. Mothers are often dismayed to find that there are no changing tables, not even in the bathroom. We explain that we find toddlers can and are helped by standing up during diaper changes, as this allows them more active participation. The mother accompanies her child to the bathroom until the child is able to go on his own.

Low shelves with toys line the walls of the toddler room and form a partial room divider for a housekeeping corner. An area rug in front of the cubbies provides space for playing on the floor and for our group circle activities. Beyond it, a long low set of tables with little chairs is used for table activities and group snack. A double easel, doll bed with dolls, small rocking chair, and two doll strollers stand to one side, a piano and bookshelf to the other side. A raised platform holds blocks, and a cupboard with drawers contains teachers' supplies. The floor-to-ceiling windows and glass door make up one wall and afford a view of and entry to the playground. The playground has several trees, a gardening area, outdoor equipment (slide, climbers, jungle gym, sandbox, swings, etc.), an enclosed storage building, and covered walkways for rainy days. The nursery and kindergarten pupils use the playground and also the toddler room, but not during toddler class periods.

The parents—and the mothers especially, just like their toddlers—start by checking out all these "basics" of the new environment and are only then ready to sit down with us at the table to get to know us and to learn more about the program.

Two teachers are in the Toddler Group at all times. They are Mrs. Phyllis Wapnick (she likes toddlers too!) and myself. Mrs. Virginia Steininger, whom the parents already know through their earlier school visits during intake, also spends periods in the class in order to build enough of a relationship with the mothers and toddlers so that she can substitute for

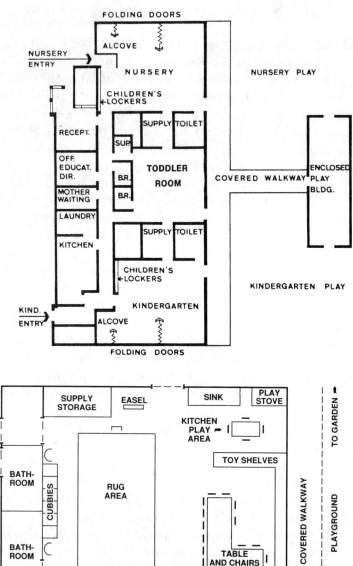

Floor Plan of the Hanna Perkins School and Toddler Room

either teacher in case of need—a rare event, but one that is anticipated and prepared for.

The teachers do not act as mother substitutes. Each mother assists her child at all times in all areas of bodily care (dressing, toileting, eating, comforting in distress). She also engages with her child in all play and activities, sits with him on the rug at circle group time, sits next to him on our little chairs at the snack table, stands or runs with him as he uses the outdoor equipment, and joins him with everyone else in ring-around-a-rosy. Should it be necessary for mother to leave her toddler briefly (to use the bathroom, to make an emergency phone call), she needs to ask a teacher to take care of him and to explain this to her child. The teacher then stays with him, helps him cope with mother's absence, hands him back to her on her return, and shares whatever may have transpired. We discuss this in terms of the toddler's need to feel safe and protected at all times from inner and outer dangers.

The parents receive the year's school calendar and an outline of our activities.

Hanna Perkins
Toddler Group

1989–1990 Calendar

First day of class	Thursday, November 2
Thanksgiving—no class	Thursday, November 23
Winter recess:	
Last class before recess	Thursday, December 21
First class after recess	Thursday, January 4
Spring break:	
Last class before break	Thursday, April 5
First class after break	Tuesday, April 17
Last class of school year	Thursday, June 28

The activities are regular and structured, yet flexible enough so that a little extra time can be allowed to extend an

ACTIVITY SCHEDULE

9:30–9:55	Greeting children and parents. Place coats, etc., in child's cubby identified by name and special color. Free play; small muscle activities, puzzles, peg board, blocks with accessories and kitchen/doll corner. Special project.
9:55–10:00	Inform children, almost time for clean up, finish what they are doing.
10:00–10:15	Clean up song, "Everybody Clean Up." Wash hands. Snack time.
10:15–10:30	Story-time; finger play and song. Picture story book and conversation.
10:30–10:50	Dress for outdoor play, wait by door. Large muscle play, trikes, wagon, seesaw, etc., and sandbox.
10:50–10:55	Tell children it's almost time to go home. Finish their play.
10:55–11:00	Put toys and equipment away, dismissal. Goodbye Song.

Let's say goodbye, goodbye, goodbye,
Let's say goodbye all together.
Let's say goodbye, goodbye, goodbye,
Let's say goodbye to each other.

engrossing and enjoyable free-play period or teacher-prepared activity; an especially tasty snack or social snack time; a new song at circle time; or nice weather for outdoor activities. The regularity of the sequences, with transitions anticipated with a special song, and carried through with an appropriate activity, such as cleaning the table before and after a snack, all help to avoid surprises and to facilitate integration and mastery. Toddlers learn to know the days of their classes, either with the aid of a weekly paper chain at home (a link severed each night and Toddler Group days marked in a special color, or by mastering the week's alternate "go–don't go" rhythm: Monday, don't go; Tuesday, go; Wednesday, don't go; Thursday, go; Friday, don't go, and then the weekend, which is usually already known as different and special. This method was invented by some of the toddlers.

As much as possible, there are no other surprises either. Some mothers are, from the start, aware of toddlers' extreme sensitivity to changes and new faces, and appreciate our consideration of this. There are no one-way mirrors or other observation facilities, nor visits by adults or children who are not a direct part of the program. Fathers and participating therapists begin to visit after some weeks of the initial adjustment period. They visit one at a time, for half-hour periods. Their visits are marked in advance on our monthly visitor schedule which the mothers check in order to prepare their children. Each visitor is introduced to everyone. Whereas fathers move around the room with mother and child, therapists usually sit next to the cubbies on one of our two adult size "big orange chairs." A child may invite a therapist to join our snack or to stand by to watch a special activity, but even then these visits are low key, congenial, and unobtrusive.

The big orange chairs also have another function. Mothers always ask worriedly at some point during open house what they would do, or where they would go, if their child acts up or even has a tantrum. Although they initially don't believe us, we assure them that, even if it takes them a longer time, with preparation, toddlers usually can be helped to do the required thing by appealing to their wish to feel good when they do well, giving them an opportunity for active participation, and clear trusting expectation. But when a child is really distressed or overwhelmed, he needs mother's containment and calming at a bit of a distance from the rest. At these times, it is generally sufficiently helpful for mother to sit with her child in one of those chairs. We have no isolation rooms, nor do we send children home. On rare occasions a child is so troubled and/or so much better calmed away from the group for a brief time that we make available the waiting room across the hall from the toddler's room, where the mothers and toddlers also wait for the start of class if they arrive early.

Often mothers ask about the participation of other members of the family: Can fathers, grandparents, or others bring the toddler instead of mother, and can siblings visit? In regard to the former question, yes, we do allow close and familiar relatives to substitute, but only for special reasons and with prior discussion and preparation, and only when it seems appropriate and helpful for the child. For example, a father has brought his child when mother needed to attend an older sibling's school function; fathers and grandparents have substituted for longer periods during the mother's confinement after the birth of a baby or during an illness. Although some mothers work outside the home, substituting is not acceptable to accommodate mother's working hours or other than immediate family commitments. As to the question of siblings' visits, the answer is no. We have learned from our early limited experience with special occasions, that siblings, older or younger, do not benefit from joining the Toddler Group, create too much conflict for their toddler brother or sister, and become an interference for the rest of the group. However, siblings who currently attend our nursery school or kindergarten are briefly greeted by mother and toddler at their playground doors when our outside period begins. One could not expect them to see her through their windows without making direct contact.

A regular open house topic has to do with the ways in which mothers can prepare their toddlers for entry. We suggest they explain that it is their very own school, where mommies never leave them, and always take care of them; that they describe the bathroom, snack, and cubby arrangements, and give their child the strip of colored paper which we prepare and which matches each child's cubby color. It will be their own color and they will mark everything they make with that color so it will be kept safe for them. Children should certainly know that there will be toys and things to do, but also that each thing is done in its turn and that, to start with, Mommy will always tell them what comes next. Other mothers and toddlers will be there too. And there are two teachers, Mrs. Furman and Mrs. Wapnick, who will help them learn such things as songs and prepare special activities, such as making playdough, to enjoy together. Mothers are encouraged to describe us to their children as they see us and as they feel their toddlers would view us, depending on the children's past experiences with other adults.

We stress that the toddlers should be informed about my accent, which may seem strange to them. This enables the mothers to voice their awareness of my accent and their curiosity about it. When I explain my ethnic background, they decide how to put it to their child. Some say, "Oh, I'll say you talk like the clerk at our supermarket." Others say, "I'll say you talk a bit different because you lived in another place when you were little." Others decide on: "Mrs. Furman kinda talks funny but she's okay." This then leads to discussion of what else might be different about any parent or child and how we should prepare the children for and address a difference in due time. The wording of these explanations is decided on primarily by the parent and child concerned. Again, some mothers are already aware of their toddlers' astute perception of and concern about even the most minor differences, such as a tiny scratch or a Band-Aid on another's finger. In our groups, some of the more striking differences have included a mother's obvious pregnancy, a trachiotomy scar, a tattoo design on her forearm, or bandage on her hand, different racial characteristics, individual food allergies which required special snacks, a child's bluish lip color due to a heart ailment, a difficulty with coordination due to a neurological weakness. There is also the question of names, such as different surnames of mother and child, or of mother and father, which alert the toddlers to family circumstances different from their own, and are sometimes anxiety arousing, such as divorce or a single-parent situation. To an extent we solve this problem by omitting last names and addressing all parents only in terms of the parental function they fulfill in the Toddler Group; for example, "Kevin's Mommy" and "Kevin's Daddy." Even so, as the year progresses, fathers' visits, or the lack of them, bring such issues to the fore and youngsters may also share news of distressing events in their lives which all hear. It is the inevitable consequence of entering the wider community of the group, and we discuss these concerns as help-fully as possible when they arise.

This first discussion of these topics and of the parents' other questions and concerns makes a starting point for think-ing them through later as they come up in their day-to-day details and ramifications. We feel it has been a good start if we succeed in conveying that our high and sometimes strange seeming expectations grow out of our appreciation of the mother–child relationship and respect for the toddlers' person-alities, and serve to support their capacities to integrate, master, and grow.

At the open house, this is further underlined as we discuss the goals of our joint work: (1) We aim to assist the child with the developmental task of achieving substantial self-care in all areas of bodily needs, learning to dress himself, eat, toilet, wash, and keep himself safe. Since these are, after all, the mother's responsibility, we contribute through our curriculum, rather than by actually doing these activities for or with the toddler. (2) We aim to help with the development of inner controls, especially in dealing with the material and social environment of the class. This includes recognizing, tolerating, and verbaliz-ing feelings; learning how to cope with frustrations; and ac-cepting delays or substitute gratifications, such as taking care of toys and taking turns. It also includes learning to be kind to others and learning to interact with peers. Here again, mothers are the main helpers, but teachers contribute as well and more directly than with bodily care. (3) We want to help the children to learn to relate to an additional person who is not a mother substitute or family member, but one who has a specific func-tion; that is, the building of the teacher–pupil relationship (E. Furman, 1986, 1987). (4) In this capacity teachers will introduce skills and activities and foster their enjoyment and mastery. The teachers help with this goal by making individually appro-priate toys and materials available and by helping with their use, as well as by inviting the children to join in prepared proj-ects, such as various craft activities, baking, cooking, and gar-dening. And they will expect participation in the only fully structured period, the group circle time for songs, rhymes, and stories. (5) We expect to prepare the toddlers, in all these areas, for their next developmental phase and entry to nursery school.

As we stress the mothers' involvement throughout and trust that they will enjoy working on these goals with their youngsters, we imply our most important goal, namely to assist mother and child to be in tune with each other.

Chapter 2

The Educational Curriculum

The educational goals, outlined to the parents at the Open House, underlie all our practices. Our weekly teachers' meeting, before and after class discussions, conferences with therapists and parents, as well as entire staff seminars, all are geared to assure that what we do and the way we do it supports each child's and his parents' growth and assists them in working toward these goals. They are the developmental tasks of the toddler phase.

BODILY SELF-CARE

Bodily self-care means that the child knows his needs and is able to take care of them independently to a sufficient extent. Years of experience with toddlers have taught us that this mastery, and the process that leads to it, are the very cornerstone of the toddler phase. For this reason, learning self-care takes up a major part of our time and activities, and we clearly convey that we value every step toward achieving it, in whichever area. This is in contrast to most toddler programs, and especially mother–toddler programs, which tend to focus on play, exercise, interests and activities, and fit in the meeting of bodily needs as quickly as possible during transition periods, almost regretting having to spend time on them at all.

Dressing and Undressing

These activities start the day, with the toddler learning to own and use his own space for his clothes and belongings. He takes off and hangs up his jacket in his cubby. With Toddler Group beginning in the fall and heading into a long cold winter, hat, snowpants, boots, and mittens are added in time and afford much opportunity for practicing the difficult tasks of dressing and undressing. We stand by, appreciating every bit of effort, pointing out how good it feels to work so hard at something, to do one's own thing, to succeed even part way. Often mother and child are still at the point of mother disregarding the child's space by stuffing her own coat into his cubby (instead of the hall closet) and the child letting her take off and care for his coat as if he were a mannikin. Or the child may run off to the toys and make her chase after him and struggle to pull off his coat. Here we might mention that: "Soon Johnny will want to be a bigger boy and take care of his own coat. We know he is a smart boy and will be very good at learning how to do it and Mommy will be glad to help." A jacket that is independently taken off and hung up deserves a special moment's pride and admiration as we take time to stand back to look at it. Eventually, when everyone has succeeded, we all celebrate the youngsters' hard won achievement as we survey the neat row of hung-up clothes. The same valuing and even more time are accorded to dressing for our outdoors period. Sometimes a child already knows the time-honored way of spreading out his jacket upside down on the floor, slipping in his arms, and tossing it backwards over his head to get it on, and emerges with a beaming expression or, as one little boy did, a proudly blurted out, "congratulations" to himself. With others we offer to demonstrate this self-help method when it seems that mother and child want help. Sometimes a child quickly copies another's successful method, showing just how aware they are of each other, even though they do not seem to be.

Since the toddlers often regard mother's selected clothing items as her arbitrary imposition, we spend every first part of our circle time on letting them figure out what to wear, and why it should be worn. Using a big feltboard with cut-outs, the children gauge the day's weather and put up the appropriate symbols. Then, using the shape of a person, they "dress" it in the order in which they dress, by putting on it each required item—snowpants, jacket with zipper, boots, hat, scarf, mittens, often checking back to see what is in their own cubbies. Rainy days are wonderful because we can even add an umbrella. This activity is usually followed by a song or rhyme with movements related to the day's weather (a snow, rain, or wind song) and/or one that helps the children with knowing and using parts of their bodies. When we became aware that many toddlers refuse to put on mittens because they cannot yet know their hands without seeing them, we added activity songs to help with that (e.g., the "mitten song": Thumbs in the thumb place, fingers all together, that's the way we do it in cold mitten weather). In addition, we have dolls that can be dressed and undressed, as well as the customary zipping and buttoning frames.

Best of all, the toddlers usually quickly extend their newly valued interests to the home. They insist on practicing their dressing skills there, help with choosing their clothes, check the weather before they leave home, or watch it with mother during the car ride to school, then proudly share what they have learned. When it gets warmer, late in our academic year, most children have mastered the basics of dressing and can take it for granted, but at that time of year they are always disappointed that there are so few items to put on our feltboard figure. Throughout, the teachers do not directly help with dressing and, on the rare occasions when mother or child ask us to take over, we refuse, saying that this is really a "Mommy job" and will in the end work out best when it is learned with Mommy's help. We know that such requests stem from specific difficulties, such as the mother's diffidence or fear of becoming too angry, or the child's rejection of mother and wish to hurt her feelings by turning to a "better" mommy.

Eating

Eating is focused around our group midmorning snack. Even though some toddlers may still use a bottle at home, during class they use their skills in self-feeding and drinking from a cup. But we aim at helping them learn much more. The teachers plan each snack for a month in advance, gauging the children's and mothers' readiness to include new tastes (such as honey from a honeycomb, less familiar fresh fruits and vegetables); items which require new skills (such as spreading peanut butter, cream cheese, or jelly on crackers with a knife); foods which are prepared by the teacher at the table (such as scraping carrots and cutting them into rounds, peeling oranges to make a "star" and dividing them into slices). There are foods that the children prepare (instant pudding, peanut butter candy balls, popcorn which they shuck from cobs, sugar cookies which we bake in the kitchen in the children's special low oven). There are foods that utilize our gardening activities (cream cheese with green onions planted and harvested in our vegetable plot; carrots for growing carrot tops in a shallow dish with water; orange and grapefruit seeds that we plant after eating the fruit, and watch as they grow into little trees to take home). We eat other fruits with different types of seeds, which we also plant for comparative study. In addition, juice and milk are served in small covered plastic pitchers with a pouring spout, from which the children themselves pour their own drink. This is in itself quite a challenge for the child, which he masters by learning to coordinate the use of both hands, and to control his wish to mess. It is a challenge to the mother, too, as she learns to support and appreciate with us her child's ability to do this for himself, instead of her doing it for him.

The snack foods are prepared in the kitchen, across the hall from the toddler room. Each child, with his mother and a teacher, takes his turn fetching the snack cart, passing out the pitchers and cups, serving the baskets or dishes with food, and in the end, wheeling the cart back again. A snack chart, listing the children's colors with their names in the same order as the sequence of their cubbies, shows whose turn it is. Since it is a highly prized activity, requiring much learning, and contributing greatly to the building of self-esteem through achievement, the toddlers and mothers keep close track of whose turn it is and anticipate it eagerly or, at times of trouble, with apprehension. No child is made to perform the task. If he refuses or otherwise indicates his unwillingness, for example, by dawdling, we say we are sorry that he makes himself miss out, hope he and Mom will work on the trouble that gets in the way, and that he will soon give himself a chance to feel good about doing his job.

Going to the kitchen, for snacks and to bake occasionally, also involves meeting our cook. She is everyone's respectful friend and the good smells and food that come from her kitchen add to her welcome. Whereas at the start the "field trip" to this new person and place can be difficult, in time the children are happy to look for her, inquire what she might be cooking for the older children's lunch, thank her for preparing our snack, and often spontaneously set aside and take to her a taste of what they have cooked.

While the snack is brought in, the others choose a place next to their mother at our table, and set it by rolling up a paper napkin and sticking it through a napkin ring they have painted in their own color. The children may eat as much as they want, but may take only two of each item at a time. They ask for and pass the pitchers and food containers to and from one another, and remain in their chairs until they are finished. At first, each of these social graces is a new and hard task, the snack time does not last long, and some of it is spent on wiping up spills. But as they learn to master each step, basking in the pride of achievement and admiring support of mother and teachers, snack time turns into a major social occasion. Not only home and school foods are discussed. Many other news items are shared, and the children learn to listen and even respond to what they hear. It is also a time to pass around, look at, and talk about special things a teacher or child has brought. Most often these are nature items, flowers, rocks, acorns, shells. Snack time is also often the occasion to announce and discuss upcoming events, such as a vacation, a new gardening activity, or seasonal changes. In the latter part of the year, snack is such an enjoyable time and so well managed by the children, that we often have to cut it short regretfully after twenty-five minutes.

Birthdays, or "special" days if the actual birthday falls outside the school year, are celebrated during snack. The respective mother and child usually bring in a batch of cookies and a small "favor" for each child, including the birthday child. The favors are the same for all: a box of crayons, a bottle of bubble-blowing liquid, or stickers. The birthday child receives a gift and card from the teachers, and a Happy Birthday song from everyone. The gift is the same throughout the year, such as a batch of playdough in the child's color with cookie cutters or scissors, or a small bag with beads and strings. The cookies and favors can be provided by the school whenever a parent prefers it that way. This has not yet happened, but it is always offered. Low key though the occasion is, it is a special learning experience in coping with big and hard feelings, a triumph when proudly accomplished, and a developmental mastery unto itself.

The learning, accomplishments, and pleasure of our group snack extend sometimes to family meals at home and certainly to other parts of our curriculum, be it preparing and cooking foods, learning about and planting seeds, or painting cardboard napkin rings. Most children make enough of these rings to take home for their family or even to serve the guests at a big holiday party. Needless to say, difficulties related to eating also spread to periods other than snack; for example, one boy told us, "They want to eat you all up" as we looked at a picture of a raccoon, and another was terrified by the phrase "open up your little mouth" in an activity song. But snack itself highlights such interferences and these are recognized and taken up in treatment-via-the-parent. They may relate to eating problems as well as to other areas, such as messing or holding back. Not surprisingly, snack time is often also using-the-toilet time.

Toileting

Unlike dressing and eating, toileting does not constitute a special period. Each child needs to learn to gauge his own body signals and attend to them in his time. Toileting and all that relates to it is nevertheless a major part of the curriculum and is certainly much on the toddlers' minds. Anal and urethral concerns, in all their stages and vicissitudes, show in the youngsters' attitudes to potentially messy activities; in their handling of the snack pitchers and watering of plants; in the way they go about using and putting away toys; in their dawdling, struggles, or open protests in response to requests; as well as in direct relation to eliminating. Mothers are often unaware of these many varied and changing manifestations and one of the ways teachers help is to point them out to mother and child or to share them with mother privately. For example, Mary may not want to paint because she got a bit worried about messing with the paints last time. That it is very nice she is starting to want to be clean and will in time be able to paint without messing, but for now we will help her with it and she will feel good making a nice picture. Or that Jimmy wiggled so much in his chair before he got so angry at Mommy, that perhaps it was hard to let himself know about needing to pee-pee and he was even a bit angry at himself. Soon he would let himself know and want to take care of it himself, be a clean boy, and then would not have to fight Mommy.

We support toilet mastery as opposed to toilet training (R. A. Furman, 1984). This stresses the child's active participation in all aspects: learning to gauge his own bodily signals, as opposed to mother gauging them for him; standing up and helping with clean-up when soiled, as opposed to being cleaned and changed lying down; dressing and undressing himself with the help of suitable clothes; flushing and taking part in disposing of diapers or rinsing out of underwear. Although we do not do any of this with or for the child, we note his evident or reported successes, support his pride in achievement, sympathize with failures, and express hope that he will soon be able to do better. Toilet mastery most especially implies developing an appropriate "turnaround" from the earlier pleasure in messing to liking oneself clean, and here we are more active. Cleaning up and admiring the clean and neat results are accorded special time in our period for putting away toys, for washing and drying our table before and after snack (using sponges and paper towels and singing accompanying songs). We have a rule that every toy and activity be neatly stored away before another is started, and that every mess, intentional or accidental, be cleaned away or swept up. Although cleaning provides an indirect opportunity to handle dirty things, we take care that cleaning does not deteriorate into messing. For example, we make sure that the child squeezes out his soapy sponge properly and really scrubs the table clean, instead of swishing the sponge around in the water, dripping it on the floor, and perhaps flooding the table surface.

Experience has also shown us that children do not benefit from displaced messing in the school setting because this is more likely to seduce them into messing than it is to encourage constructive pursuits. For this reason we do not provide such activities as fingerpainting, but help the children use potentially messy media, such as paints, glue, sand, and earth, to make things. For example, we encourage making sandpies while sitting at the edge board of the sandbox, instead of lying in the sand and throwing it around. We also provide implements for using these media so that they do not get directly on the hands: brushes to apply paint or glue only in the right place, and a small dipper to ladle earth into plant pots. We always have a moist sponge handy, so that the child can wipe off his fingers when they get so dirty that either his wish to mess or a beginning dislike of it threaten to interfere with working at the task. Of course, the child's affect determines, above all, when, how, or whether the teacher would intervene. One child may get into quite a mess while painting but his intent is calmly focused on pursuing his activity; another child may barely scribble a mark off the paper, but his excitement in messing shows in his suddenly twinkling eyes, facial expression, and jerky movements. The goal is to help the child's self remain in control.

Although toileting is private, mothers and toddlers are very aware of each child's progress, or lack of same. When a child uses the bathroom on his own for the first time, there is sometimes a hushed moment of awed silence, followed by comments of proud comparison with himself ("I did pee-pee in the toilet at home") or by looks of shame, or by defensive maneuvers, such as changing the subject. We may say that we know everyone is trying to be clean on his or her own, that it's very nice for Chris to know how to do that already, but we are sure each boy or girl will make it and feel good.

Washing Oneself

This comes up as part of cleaning, and washing one's own hands is a valued, hard-won achievement. Often this activity prompts the toddler to talk of learning to wash himself in the tub at home or of hating having his hair washed. Such discussions afford opportunities to alert the mother to an area of difficulty or to support her efforts at home. Washing himself and *sleeping* (for which there is no period in our program) are also introduced by way of books, pictures, and songs. For example, our daily "Mice song" has everyone act out the sequences of sleeping, waking, washing, eating (at the children's request we included brushing teeth). Such favorites as the *I Can Do It By Myself* book (Goldsborough, 1981) or *Big Beds and Little Beds* (Seymour, 1965) lead into a discussion of who does what by himself, including settling himself down to sleep. Not so long ago, when a little boy proudly listed all he does for himself, his mother reminded him, "But you still have to work on helping yourself to go to sleep!"

Keeping Safe

Keeping safe, protesting pain, and seeking and accepting comfort are a crucial part of self-care, and, although we expect some aspects to have been mastered during the first year, their age-appropriate progress is much valued and supported as well as taught in Toddler Group. Our basic rule is clearly stated and kept: "This is a safe place. Everybody and everything has to be safe here." The safety rule applies to outer as well as inner safety. We stress the goal for the child to learn to gauge his own safety and we value and encourage his "being safe and kind to himself," be it by steering clear of obstacles or of an angry peer, sitting safely, not running heedlessly, alerting mother to hurts or not feeling well, and staying with mother so that she can help him be safe. When the child is not safe, we show concern, help him see what went wrong, and hope he will soon want to take good care of himself. When mother does not gauge the child's safety sufficiently, we alert her and ask her to intervene before a hurt occurs. If necessary, we take over and then hand her child back to her as quickly as possible. We similarly help the child and mother to look out for the inner danger of getting out of control, perhaps too excited or aggressive in his play, which will not make him feel safe with himself, or may lead to acting unsafely. With toddlers, inner and outer unsafety often go together. An overwhelmed child may dissolve into a tantrumlike anxiety, and require calming by mother, and then help in finding an activity that will restore his good feeling of being in control. He may also become bodily unsafe or behave in an excited–aggressive way with mother, peers, or toys.

Being unsafe with or toward others, as in aggressive acts aimed at them, their space, or belongings, is not only forbidden because it is unkind to them, but because it makes the attacker feel unsafe. "If we let you hurt him, you would think that we would also let him hurt you. We help to keep everyone safe." Teachers, of course, don't hurt the children, but neither can mothers do so in Toddler Group. Toys and equipment likewise cannot be mistreated or aggressively misused. If damaged, they must be fixed and/or set aside until the next time, "When you will have another chance to show yourself that you can use it in a good and safe way." Even the occasional unwelcome insect is not killed but picked up by the teacher with a moist sponge and released outside. Given the toddlers' tendency not to differentiate themselves from other people, from animals or even things, all-round safety as a way of being kind and feeling good is helpful to them. We have learned that even youngsters who were very aggressive to others in the home or in other groups show minimal aggression in our setting because they feel protected, from themselves and others. Another reason for this is that keeping safe is viewed as kindness to oneself, whereas elsewhere or before it may have seemed like an imposition to please the adults. Being unsafe may have been the child's way of provoking or angering adults. At the same time, our setting enables us more readily to pinpoint interferences with being safe with oneself and/or with recognizing hurts, problems that have often escaped the attention they warrant.

DEVELOPMENT OF INNER CONTROLS

It may seem that a great deal is expected of our toddlers, that this would bring many frustrations, and stress their capacities for inner controls. In some respects this is true, but with each child the expectations are timed and graded to reflect his inner readiness and expectations of himself as well as to his mother's ability to be in tune with that part of him. A mother easily mistakes her toddler's struggle over being dressed for angry contrariness, but misses out on recognizing his underlying wish to do it himself, or his feelings of anger and inadequacy at not being able to do it as well as she does. Often indeed, a child needs help in setting lower standards for himself or reassurance that he will soon achieve his aims. With the development of inner controls, as with self-care, the emphasis throughout is on his good feeling about himself when he tries or succeeds, as opposed to criticism or reprimand for not trying or succeeding. The repeated experience of pleasure in working toward mastery is a self-motivating force and makes each task, each step within a task, satisfying rather than a chore.

Facilitating Mastery

The children's ability to cope with inner and outer stimuli is further greatly helped by our efforts to make them masterable (integratable). Rules are simple, clear, and consistent. The reasons for them make sense in terms of protecting the child's own safety and well-being and apply to everyone, including the adults—perhaps especially the adults, because the child identifies with what we do rather than with what we say. As already mentioned, we adapt our activities to the toddlers' stimulation tolerance (no big parties or overwhelming field trips, no unnecessary changes, no coming and going of observers), and we carefully prepare them for all events.

Mastery is also facilitated by our observing reality with them and helping them understand it, not only the nice and undisturbing aspects of reality, but the many upsetting, confusing, or, for the adult, unwelcome aspects of reality which are often glossed over. This may include hard feelings and inner struggles on the one hand, or their observations of the world around them, on the other hand—be it my wrinkles, a dead worm, another's bodily anomaly, troubled behavior, or absence from the group. No topic is taboo. Sometimes only a look or a transient facial expression betray a child's deep concern. For example, one day, while getting ready to play ring-around-a-rosy, white-skinned Mary happened to line up so as to hold black-skinned Marjorie's hand. A shadow of bewilderment crossed Mary's face as she looked at the outstretched hand, and then she clasped it. Marjorie looked at Mary's face blankly. Then both children joined in the game. I shared my observation with both mothers privately. They had not noticed. Their children did not say anything about it at home. It was not until the next time, when I discussed it sympathetically with each of the mother–child couples, that the children could acknowledge feelings of "yukky-dirty" and "not liked" respectively. With Mary a simple clarification afforded relief; for Marjorie it opened up a painful topic with many ramifications.

Feelings and Impulses (Manifestations of Urges)

Assistance with mastery and intellectual understanding are not used to eliminate the attending feelings but to help the child experience them in a manageable form, and, whenever possible, in relation to the inner or outer situation which arouses them. Some toddlers are still at the stage of responding to inner turmoil by experiencing bodily sensations or discharging motorically. Their mothers may support this, telling the child and us that he is "tired," "hungry," "has a bit of a cold," or that he is "hyper" today or "contrary for no reason." Here mother and child need help with recognizing feelings and assisting the child in knowing and naming them. Some toddlers do experience feelings mentally, but may need help in other ways: in differentiating them, relating them to the appropriate context, containing them, expressing them in words rather than in behavior, or using them to decide on an appropriate relieving action, such as asking mother for comfort when sad; when scared, asking for protection or clarifying reassurance. Some toddlers use defenses (i.e., unconscious means of warding off awareness of feelings) and need help with them to be able to face and tolerate their underlying feelings. With a manifestly very angry child, mother and he may need help in recognizing this as a way of warding off fear or feelings of inadequacy. With an overly clinging and affectionate child, mother and child may need to be alerted to the underlying anger.

As already mentioned, oral greed is not gratified but we try to help the children find more mature satisfactions in eating, such as their achievements in serving themselves and others, in being proud of learning good manners at the table, and in enjoying the social communication during mealtimes. Likewise, anal and urethral impulses, such as messing, are not directly gratified but channeled into constructive activities and valued "turnarounds" in the form of the early ideal of liking oneself clean.

With sadism, especially, we avoid stimulation (no hurting or killing of insects or plants, no sadistic stories or songs, and, of course, no sadistic behavior or attitudes on the part of adults). We are careful to promote kindness and pity, the latter being the appropriate "turnaround" to replace sadism. When a child gleefully stomps on an ant or thoroughly relishes intimidating others with his account of a sadistic TV program or event, we acknowledge and name his "hurting excitement" or "hurting fun" and intervene, telling him that we don't let anyone be unkind and that he himself will feel better about himself when, like the bigger people, he learns to enjoy different kinds of fun. If someone or something really gets hurt, we encourage the child to share our concern and efforts to comfort, rescue, or heal the afflicted. The mothers are at first usually taken aback, then privately "confess" their poisoning and spraying "rampages" at home, begin to observe their children's reactions to these more closely, and, most of the time, take it up in their sessions with the therapist, as well as joining us in our efforts. Many a family then takes a different attitude and supports their child's more humane interest in the living world. Such interests in, say, bugs, become the bridge to a "turnaround" of pity or even to an intellectual pursuit, or they may serve to explore further the nature and vicissitudes of the child's sadism.

Manifest aggression per se is of course also recognized and acknowledged. Depending on the situation, the child may need help to channel it into verbal, rather than physical expression, or to relate it to the appropriate content, or to understand its defensive use. For example, toddlers not infrequently attack and blame their mother when they are really angry at themselves, perhaps for feeling incompetent or guilty. With some children it can already represent a wish for punishment or a way of being anxious. Often it is our task to help mother and child notice the absence of appropriate anger and the means of warding it off from awareness. One boy was very angry when really worried, but could not even complain when another child's mother accidentally broke his playdough shape, or when we noticed a scratch on his arm which had been inflicted by his brother. Another boy simply became incompetent when angry and lost all zest in activities. Although the mother is often the target of the child's anger, this is also the most frequent area of conflict for the child. Excessive affection helps to ward off anger and/or it shows in a loyalty conflict between the child's liking for mother and teacher, and may lead to refusal to have anything to do with us.

Whereas such concerns over mixed feelings of love and anger may have roots in individual earlier and current home experiences, and are taken up in treatment-via-the-parent, in Toddler Group we focus on the phase-appropriate task of learning to use one's love to tame anger and to help the child know that his anger need not gain the upper hand or really cause hurt to the loved one. Toddlers are often greatly relieved to hear that we know it is scary to get so angry, but that Mommy and teachers will help with not letting them do angry things; that nobody will be angry back; that they will find their loving feelings again, and that this is easier for the grown-ups and will become easier for them. Right now it must seem strange and hard to believe that people can love them even when they are angry, but in time they too will keep their love always and then they won't have to worry so when they get angry.

Taming of anger and being considerate are also part of learning to interact with peers, asking them for a turn or a toy, making up when there has been an unkindness. We value "being kind," stress how good we can feel about ourselves when we are kind, point it out when a child has been kind, perhaps by allowing another child to share the blocks or giving him a toy after finishing with it. When a child is absent, we help the children notice and explain simply. During snack the teacher then draws a card to be sent to the one who is not with us. The children help word the message to him and are usually happy to "sign" with their color mark. These cards are always appreciated, often with spontaneous thanks, and this makes everyone feel good.

Being kind, making an effort to please another, brings valued inner rewards and furthers the developing wish to interact with peers in a friendly way. Whereas on the one hand our toddlers need help in learning to respect other children and treat them as people like themselves (and this is greatly helped by each having his mother with him and feeling safe), on the other hand it is still hard for them to differentiate themselves when a peer shows intense feelings. Here we often say that John is very sad, angry, worried, and so on, but that his Mommy will help him to feel better, and it is not the other child's feeling. Sometimes, of course, it is their feeling, in instances where a child projects, vicariously enjoys, or criticizes his own feelings as vested in another, and this too needs to be addressed.

Toddlers' sensitivity to the behavior of others is also or perhaps especially marked in regard to excitement. Therefore, for the child's own and the others' sake, we alert mothers when their child masturbates and suggest that she discuss with him the need for privacy. Some forms of self-stimulation may be evident only to a very minor extent but may get in the way of doing activities or sitting safely. In these instances we may point out that one really can't do two things at the same time, that the child would probably feel better if he could do his "school things" properly, but if he really wants to choose wiggling, he would have to do it in the bathroom because this is our only private place. Sometimes a child's excitement shows in sensuous ways of touching mother's body or pushing into father's crotch. Such behaviors may go unrecognized by the parents, but can be shown to them by the way they affect the child, namely leading to an inability to focus on activities, to increasing loss of behavioral control, even tantrums. In these instances, helping the child gauge what becomes "too exciting and then isn't fun any more" requires much tact in talking privately with parent and child, with the emphasis on enabling the child to feel in control of himself.

THE TEACHER–CHILD RELATIONSHIP

As already discussed, we avoid being mother substitutes, do not take over mother's role, do not intrude into the mother–child relationship, and do not pose as "better Mommies." To start with, we always address mother and child together, do not "seduce" the child by offering him toys or activities he might like, but allow mother and child to choose what they wish. When there is a need to intervene—perhaps to ensure safety, to show how something works, or to prepare for the next period—we tend to talk to mother in such a way that the child feels included and can understand but is not directly confronted and is assured that mother remains in charge. We might say, for example, "Timmy's Mommy, we shall soon sing our cleaning-up-toys song. You might want to remind Timmy about that so that he can get ready to finish his puzzle." We may be more direct in appreciating something a child has worked at or accomplished, conveying what we value, and sharing a positive moment. Gauging mother's and child's readiness, we may later offer to display a nice painting in our "gallery" in the hallway where the nursery and kindergarten children also have their areas for display (it takes a long time before a child is ready to keep his productions at school, as this implies a real investment in us and the group). We may offer to introduce a different way of using a toy or suggest a more challenging one; we may sit by and admire a block building in progress, or ask if we may join in a pretend tea party. With teacher-prepared projects at our table, mother and child join us when the child wishes to.

Our care in approaching the child is prompted by respect for his limited capacity to integrate new things and people and by our first needing to understand how he views us. Toddlers who are not sufficiently in touch with their mothers may approach and/or disregard us without actually thinking of us as individuals different from mother. With them, helping the mother–child relationship is the first goal, and only when this is well under way, do they respond to us selectively. Most youngsters, however, are very clear on that score. They regard us as potential mother substitutes, sitters, or family members like the ones who have taken care of them. This shows in the many variations of their almost ubiquitous loyalty conflict, but surfaces in other ways too. For example, going home at the end of class is often most unwelcome. For some children it represents a rejection, in part because the idea of a time-limited relationship is still new to them. Martin had several days of tantrums at leaving time, in spite of preparation. Encouraged to tell his mother why it was so hard, he finally yelled at her, "Throw you out!" I intervened here, explaining to mother and Martin that he was angry at us and felt we were throwing him out, didn't want him with us any longer. He looked wide-eyed as I added that we too are sorry our time is over, that teachers and children always have only a play and learning time together, and then all of us have to say good-bye and go to our own homes until it is Toddler Group time again. Along with helping to sort out misunderstandings, we also convey our understanding of the child's thinking and feeling, and our support of his wish to master. This builds our relationship with him.

As the year progresses, the children come to enjoy more direct interactions and the learning relationship with us. They eagerly investigate our prepared projects on arrival, turn to us with appropriate questions, share their own knowledge and experiences, and become thoroughly engaged in working with us. The pleasure in activities and in understanding and mastering inner and outer reality with a teacher has begun. However, just as the earlier difficulties with learning about the teacher relationship are overcome, new ones surface, now often representing more advanced concerns over bodily differences and adequacy, albeit in indirect form; for example, envy of the teacher's knowledge and/or feelings of inadequacy in regard to the child's own performance. The teacher does not link these manifestations to their bodily origins. We alert mother to them, but with the child we focus on helping him recognize his feeling and using it to master the task at hand. "I can understand that you would like to be the one to read the story. It can make us angry when we don't yet know how to do something. But right now you will feel a lot bigger and better if you can listen like a big Toddler Group boy and in time you will learn to read too." Sometimes both the earlier and later interferences are by-products of developmental conflicts, readily clarified and redirected. At other times they are surface manifestations of deeper and more widespread problems to be worked on in therapy.

The Teachers' Relationship with the Mothers

Often mothers, too, need help in defining our role for themselves. In inner "sync" with their toddler, they may feel a bit like a toddler themselves. On the one hand, this helps them to enjoy the activities, interactions, and protective containing environment; on the other hand, it may tempt them to want to be mothered, rather than to mother (e.g., getting so busy singing songs with us as to forget to look out for their child's feeling or behavior), or to become contrary and "forget" our rules (e.g., a mother may so much want to do "her own thing" that she may disregard our rule as well as her child's safety, allow him to climb a ladder too high, and get hurt slipping or falling off). At times a mother may even prefer to be the teacher instead of the mother, perhaps taking charge of the easel and paints for other children, while neglecting to attend to her own toddler. We work toward establishing the kind of relationship with the mother which, above all, supports her mothering, helps and appreciates her ability to understand and feel with her child, and helps him to master; and empathizes with the hardship this often involves. In this context she then assists her child in our joint efforts to help him care for his body, to relate to us as teachers, and to invest pleasurably in the activities and skills we offer. For many mothers it brings back happy moments from their own childhood, for many more it is their first opportunity to share in such pursuits, which they often speak to, and which makes Toddler Group such a rich and enjoyable period for them. It also makes leaving Toddler Group hard.

The Relationship with Fathers

The teachers' relationships with the toddlers' fathers are built in part indirectly, via the mother's and child's accounts to the fathers of what transpires in class, via the changes in behavior and attitudes which are carried over into the home, and via the fathers' participation in the treatment-via-the-parent. But in part these relationships are built directly through our meeting at the initial open house and the twice yearly evaluation conferences (see below), through scheduled visits in class, and, in some instances, fathers' occasional or prolonged substituting for mother under special circumstances, as discussed earlier. Throughout we convey not only that we welcome fathers, but appreciate their importance to mother and child as fathers, rather than as mere second or substitute mothering persons. We stress the father's helpfulness in supporting the mother's day-to-day work with their child as well as his role in building the family threesome of mother-father-child to succeed the earlier twosome. We share our observations of the child's special and different relationship and behavior with his father. We value fathers' observations of their child, in class and at home, which often contribute new aspects and lead to a better understanding of the child as well as of the mother–child relationship. And, by alerting the mother to her child's responses to other fathers' visits, we often help her become aware of his longing for his father. Especially in cases where the father has been less involved with his child at home or has not made time to visit, or is actually not in the home through divorce, single parenting, or foster parent care, these observations have brought about both parents' better understanding of the father's importance. This has resulted in renewed or closer contact with the father and in Toddler Group visits which became highlights in the child's and also the father's lives, and were turning points in personality growth and family relationships. Such occasions affect the whole group and underline the important role of fathers also for those families which have taken their fathers for granted. Thus, in spite of limited direct contact, and in spite of the fathers' frequent feeling that they don't count for much with the young child, or that, by way of projection, we will not consider them important, fathers come to feel respected and affirmed in their real role with the child and the mother–child relationship (R. A. Furman, 1983; E. Furman, 1987).

INTRODUCING THE ENJOYMENT AND MASTERY OF SKILLS AND ACTIVITIES

Toddlers between the ages of 18 months to 3 years vary enormously in their readiness to engage in the use of neutral, that is, bodily and instinctually nongratifying activities, and in their capacity to learn the related skills. At the same time, each child's progress through this phase is marked by equally enormous and rapid strides when parents and teachers support these developments. The group variation and individual changes in these areas are usually much greater than in later phases. The teacher therefore has to have available a much greater variety of equipment, and gear its introduction much more closely to the individual child's needs. Yet, all toddlers' integrative capacities are limited, so that care has to be taken not to overwhelm them by presenting them with too many things and too many choices. Since the toddlers as well as their mothers are often not too good at gauging readiness and appropriate progressive steps, they need much help. Some children and mothers underestimate what the child can do, others overestimate, and with still others, the child underestimates and the mother overestimates, or vice versa. It is not uncommon for mother and child to avoid even the simplest puzzle, or to persist in using the same beginning three-piece inset puzzle, or to start and get frustrated with a thirty-piece unframed puzzle. Alternately, mother and child may get into a conflict as one chooses too easy a puzzle and the other too hard a one, or neither of them knows how to progress from an easier to a suitably harder one.

Selection and Use of Toys

To start with, we have relatively few toys and activities available and make sure there are some toys and activities of which there are several sets, some of which there are two, and some of which there is only one, and perhaps a comparable but not identical set. We gauge this on the basis of our experience with which toys are initially most often preferred and our preliminary knowledge, through intake, of each child's interests and level of development. We offer less identical items of the more advanced toys, not only because less children will use them but because those who do are usually also more ready to learn to wait for a turn or to accept a substitute activity—lessons in frustration tolerance and social interaction. Close observation and discussion at our weekly teachers' meeting help us know when to add new toys, which child might be just ready for the next step, or when the group as a whole can absorb more materials. When an individual child is ready for a next step, say using a less thick crayon or smaller beads to thread, we may offer it then and there. When most of the group is ready for something new, we prepare in advance and usually start with the teacher using it; for example, small building blocks or sewing cards. We take it for granted that it is not the toy or activity in itself, but the sharing of the loved adult's pleasure in using it which fosters the child's interest.

We select toys and materials which can be used in a variety of ways and avoid those which do things themselves in an inevitably circumscribed mechanical manner, such as toys activated by push buttons, dolls which walk and talk, cars which run a stretch. These do nothing to engage the child's creativity, to foster his wish for mastery through effort, or to challenge his quest for understanding. By contrast, even the simple pegboard with colored pegs—most often the first and most beloved toy in Toddler Group—lends itself to test finger muscle strength, to figure out how to remove pegs in different ways by pulling or pushing through, and to arrangements by different colors and patterns. Often we assist by admiring a new way a child uses a toy, or by pointing out a new way he might use it, or by encouraging him to figure out why his way does not work and what he could do to change it to achieve his goal. Valuing and supporting the child's individual thinking and approaches to toys is especially important in helping him invest his own function and in helping his mother to appreciate it instead of "showing him how." With a new or more difficult puzzle, for example, it is almost irresistible for mothers to teach the child their way of doing it, such as finding the corner pieces, or matching color pieces, and putting in some pieces themselves. When we point out that there are hundreds of individual ways of going about it, and that it is fun for child, mother, and teacher to discover his own way, mothers are usually disbelieving at first, then become fascinated. More than once, a mother has exclaimed in amazement, "My goodness, he can really think!" and could then better assist instead of imposing.

With *symbolic play* too, many toddlers need the teacher's pleasurable investment in order to use toys creatively. Some may still largely rely on their blankie or stuffed toy from home, may not even use dolls or the kitchen corner for symbolically recreating the familiar maternal activities, such as taking the "baby" in the stroller or serving a pretend meal. Others need encouragement and participation to begin to combine different toys to create an imaginary experience; for example, by using small blocks to build stalls for each farm animal, or wooden tracks to make a road for their little cars. Some need help in containing and channeling their play to protect it from interference by excited or aggressive impulses (E. Furman, 1985a), and some need assurance that fantasy play will not get out of control and cause real effects. Sometimes the content of play, avoidance of play, or interferences with it point to conflicts within the child. We apprise the mother of this but do not interpret to the child, except perhaps to let him know that something is getting in the way of his having fun playing, or that something seems to be a worry, and that Mommy and he will work it out and that will help.

Activities, Skills, and Interests

As the relationship with us as teachers becomes established, we increasingly offer a prepared project, some of which later extend over several class periods, to introduce and practice special skills (cutting, sewing, gluing, planting) and to stimulate interests (rocks, shells, cooking). The planning of these activities takes place in our teachers' meetings, keeping in mind overall goals for the whole year, with monthly specific curricula and weekly adaptations to fit the group's and individual toddlers' needs. We aim for progression with mastery—new ideas and skills develop from previously established ones—take the children's own ideas into account, and fit in with other activity periods. For example, our feltboard weather and dressing activity at circle time, described earlier, may introduce the idea of wind and lead to a project of cutting out simple kites to use at outdoors time. Dressing and mitten songs may be followed up by tracing hands on paper and cutting out mittens. Eating carrots at snack and planting the tops to grow their feathery greens may be the start for more intricate gardening activities outdoors and also for reading *The Carrot Seed* (Krauss, 1945). Art projects too are selected so as to foster integrated understanding. Tissue paper flowers are made when we have real flowers on the table and have observed and thought about a succession of them. Suncatchers are made when we have observed the sun and the light, shadows, and warmth it provides. The things we make with the children are as much as possible not only for display but for use. This enhances their value, be it a decorated plant pot, a strung necklace, or a painted shell as a knickknack container. Although we use mostly simple household materials so that each activity can be readily repeated at home, we avoid using them just to use them; for example, we don't make the favorite preschool egg container caterpillars because most children are not familiar enough with caterpillars to recognize them in this artificial form.

We make a special point of sharing our interest in the natural world: weather, animals, plants, rocks, seasonal changes, birth, growth, and death. With plants, for example, this may start early in the year with growing carrot tops and sweet potatoes in water, and later go on to growing green onions, peas, and potatoes outdoors. We also note their decay, as our cut flowers and plantings rot and are buried in our garden, or as we watch the leaves fall off the trees and later observe them in various stages of disintegration. Many of these things are new and fascinating for the parents, too, and they pick up on our enthusiasm and do similar activities at home with the whole family.

The songs, rhymes, pictures, and books we introduce at circle time often relate to these interests or present them in another form. Here again our overall monthly and weekly planning focuses on progressive, integrated themes. We may start out with a couple of pictures of familiar pet animals, cat and dog, and go on to pictures, books, and songs about local wild animals (squirrel, chipmunk, raccoon), farm animals, and birds. We also make pinecone bird feeders with bacon grease and birdseed, show specimens of the respective nests, usually find at least some broken bird eggshells to put in them, and sort our feather collection to attach the right ones to each bird's picture. We select nursery rhymes carefully and make sure their words are understood; for example, "Twinkle, Twinkle, Little Star" usually reveals that the children not only don't know what a diamond is but have never looked at a star. This leads to helping them discover the stars (a winter project) and the moon, and even phases of the moon, and we put those up on our feltboard as well each time. Many a mother finds this intriguing, asks why the moon is sometimes up in the evening and sometimes in the morning, why the sickle faces one way or the other, and soon begins to share this new interest with her child.

As the year goes on, new interests are increasingly introduced by the children themselves. One brings in a starfish found during a spring vacation, another a colorful rock, or the beans which grew on the plant we started in class with a bean seed in a jar with cotton, or an account of a squirrel found dead by the roadside. The children's own interests are always followed up, regardless of our curriculum.

Most important, however, is not the content or integrated progression of any of these activities and interests, but the enjoyment the teacher brings to their pursuit. Her investment helps child and parent to invest them, to taste the new mental pleasures of learning, working, thinking, observing, creating, understanding, mastering; the pleasure in the process and in the achievement, pleasure worth the effort they entail, and pleasure that builds self-esteem.

GETTING IN TUNE

Earlier I mentioned that our implicit but most important goal is to assist parent and child to be in tune with one another. There are no specific prescriptions for bringing this about. It relies above all on a milieu of true respect for and empathy with the mother, the father, the child, and all of their relationships. It relies also on the professional's ability to derive pleasure and satisfaction from supporting *their* efforts. In practice this means that we do need to recognize fully, in parent as in child, their short-comings and difficulties, but focus on their strengths, appreciate their struggles to do well, and sympathize with the hardships this involves for them. When a mother lets her child wander off or a father fails to schedule a visit, they may do so because of various pathologies and interferences in their parenting, but first and foremost it means that they don't know how important they are to their child. When a child rages at his mother and refuses to do her bidding, he may likewise manifest all kinds of problems, but first and foremost, he and mother must not forget that he also loves and needs her and is frightened by the intensity of his anger. When a mother or father sense that we understand their feelings, we can help them understand the child's. Being a parent is as difficult as being a helpless toddler, in its own way. When this is acknowledged, along with the desperate wish of each to be felt with and helped to master, they can begin to feel for each other and to use the positives in themselves and in each other. A hard day deserves sympathy for mother and child, needs to be viewed as a challenge to figure out what went wrong and why, merits trusting assurance that things will work out better, but above all it is just a hard day. It is not proof of a mother's or child's badness or incompetence, it need not be an assault on the fragile self-regard of either. As one little girl once said after being scolded by her mother, "But in most ways I am very nice." The teacher can help parent and child put things in this kind of perspective.

Many a time, parents need help to recognize their child's impulses, their anger, greed, excitement, wish to mess, but most often they need help in appreciating the child's self: its anxieties, its vulnerability, its defenses. When Karen did not want to put on her hat, she was not intent on defying Mommy but on being like Mommy. Mother never wore a hat but she had never taken that into consideration, and only when alerted by us could she suddenly recall the many other ways in which Karen wanted to be like her. This not only helped them to sort out the hat struggle, but put mother in touch with her little girl's new aspirations. Although these too implied potential conflicts, mother felt flattered: "My, I didn't realize I was worth imitating!"

Getting in tune is an ongoing process. It suffers inevitable periodic setbacks, progresses more in some areas than in others, and is, no doubt, never achieved to perfection. It is greatly facilitated by the child's actual behavioral improvements which result from mother's better understanding of him. Since it is also as much the goal of the therapist's work in treatment-via-the-parent as it is the teachers' goal, it is further fueled by the parent's identification with the therapist's and teacher's nonjudgmental and empathic viewing of the child in his own right.

One way in which we enlist the parents in looking at their child as we do is the twice yearly *parent–teacher conferences*. These are prepared for by a letter handed out a month in advance in mid-January and mid-May, respectively. It explains the purpose of these conferences as an opportunity for teachers and parents to share their observations and thoughts about the child's overall functioning and progress and to discuss ways in which we can help him. The Evaluation of Progress Outline is enclosed with the letter. The Outline lists the developmental masteries as manifested in class behavior, and the levels of each mastery at which a child may function.

PROGRESS IN THE TODDLER GROUP IN AREAS OF DEVELOPMENT AND MASTERY OF TASKS

How does the toddler feel about the program?

> Has the toddler made it a meaningful part of his or her activities?
>
> Which parts of it are liked and which disliked?

Does the toddler think and talk about it at home positively or negatively?

Does the toddler want to bring ideas and things to share or to show?

Does the toddler feel pleased and proud with what has been learned or unhappy with what he or she cannot yet accomplish?

Orienting self in the group setting:

Does the toddler know his or her own color and cubby, whereabouts of exits, sink, toilet, equipment, toys?

Does the toddler know the sequence of program activities?

Does the toddler use preparation for and cope with changes, such as new activities, new participants and visitors, absences of self or of others?

Self-care:

Does the toddler want to and enjoy learning to care for self and take pride in accomplishments?

Does the toddler know parts of his or her own body?

Does the toddler recognize hurts and seek appropriate help?

Does the toddler avoid common dangers and use help to keep safe?

Does the toddler recognize and take care of his or her own clothes and belongings?

Which skills in dressing and undressing have been mastered and is the toddler eager to learn more?

Does the toddler enjoy eating at snack time, use appropriate table manners, serve self, sit at table, try new foods, share with others?

Has the toddler achieved toilet mastery or made steps toward independent toileting? Is the toddler clean and tidy with equipment, such as cleaning tables, putting away toys?

Does the toddler show exaggerated concern about cleanliness?

Relationship with teacher:

Does the toddler recognize the teachers and know their names?

Has the toddler begun to use the teacher as an additional person who introduces and assists with play and learning activities or does the toddler view the teacher as a mother substitute? Is the toddler able to like mother and teacher and to use each relationship appropriately?

Does the toddler accept the differences between home and group rules?

Does the toddler cooperate with the teacher's expectations?

Relationships with peers:

Does the toddler recognize and know peers by name?

Is the toddler aware of them but also able to differentiate self?

Does the toddler respect the rights of others, take turns, share the teacher and toys?

Does the toddler engage in parallel play, in give-and-take play?

Is the toddler beginning to show kindness and pity?

Inner controls:

How does the toddler cope with minor frustrations? Can he or she accept delays or substitutes (not this but that, not here but there, not now but later)?

Does the toddler follow routines and directions?

Does the toddler practice skills and persist in spite of failure or inadequacy, and can he or she request and use help?

Does the toddler recognize and correct mistakes?

Does the toddler recognize different feelings in self? To what extent can the toddler tolerate feelings? Can he or she express them in words?

Does the toddler recognize wrongdoing and is he or she able to make up?

Speech:

Does the toddler use words to communicate needs, feelings, ideas, experiences?

Does the toddler enjoy talking?

What is the range of the toddler's vocabulary; does he or she use single words, phrases, or sentences? Is the speech clear?

Can the toddler listen to the words of others and respond in words?

Can the toddler learn through verbal dialogue?

Observing and thinking:

Does the toddler notice the surroundings and figure them out age-appropriately and ask for clarification?

Does the toddler think before doing?

Can the toddler differentiate animate from inanimate, real from pretend (or artificial)?

Motor Control:

Large muscle control—

Is the toddler safe and age-appropriately coordinated?

Does the toddler enjoy bodily activities?

Which skills are now mastered or practiced (climbing, jumping, throwing and catching ball, pumping on swing and seesaw, balancing, tricycle riding, etc)?

Small muscle control—

Does the toddler show age-appropriate coordination and enjoyment?

Which skills has the toddler mastered or practiced (zipping, buttons, snaps, use of crayons, playdough, paints, scissors)?

Play:

Which toys and materials are used and enjoyed?

Does the toddler appreciate toys as symbols and use them creatively?

Does the toddler enjoy materials but differentiate them from bodily pleasures (e.g., is playdough or paints used without either fearing or wanting to make a mess; scissors to cut, not to attack or destroy)?

Is the toddler able to accept ideas for play or activities as well as adding his or her own?

Is the toddler interested in new playthings or activities?

Are play or activities easily interfered with by excitement, anger, fear, or frustration?

Work:

Does the toddler enjoy the process of working at a skill or activity?

Does the toddler enjoy the end product?

Does the toddler concentrate on activities and persist in mastering them?

Does the toddler accept and follow suggestions?

Does the toddler have age-appropriate expectations of self?

How does the toddler cope with mistakes or failures?

Music rhythms, and fingerplays:

Does the toddler enjoy and participate in teacher-initiated activities and/or in his or her own?

Which activities are most liked or disliked (songs, movement, fingerplays, instruments)?

Does the toddler remember and use what has been learned?

Pictures, books, and stories:

Does the toddler enjoy these activities on his or her own, with mother, and/or with the teacher and peers?

Does the toddler remember what has been seen or told?

In which ways does he or she use them—naming objects and people, understanding situations and sequences, feeling with a story or picture character?

Natural environment:

Does the toddler observe the weather?

Does the toddler learn about changes in weather and seasons?

Does the toddler observe and learn about animals?

Does the toddler observe and learn about plants?

Individual characteristics:

The toddler's special interests, likes, and dislikes;

Special concerns or fears.

Parents' and teachers' suggestions:

For furthering the toddler's growth;

For improving or adapting the program to his or her needs.

During the month prior to our meeting, the parents and teachers prepare their separate assessments. The categories are never rigidly adhered to and no check list is made, but we take care to address all areas, and the parents add much more. They compare and relate school and home behavior, bring their thinking on areas of difficulty, ask us about ways of handling situations, share our pleasure in progress, and plan for the next steps. Since most parents keep the first Outline and use it on their own through the rest of the year, it provides a guideline to focus their observations and ours on the same issues, at least in regard to the child's growth in Toddler Group.

TRANSITION TO NURSERY SCHOOL

Knowing that ending Toddler Group and entering Nursery School is hard, not least because it represents the transition for mother and child from one developmental phase to a new one, we take special care to prepare for this. The parents usually agonize over it some months ahead, the children inevitably tune in on the parents' concerns, and therapists and teachers deal with them individually as they arise.

Group Preparation

The group preparation begins about six weeks before the end of the school year with a letter to the parents outlining the steps: First the parents need to arrange a visit in the Nursery School without their child; then the Nursery School teachers visit individually in the Toddler Group, usually during a snack period; last, the mother schedules a Nursery School visit with her child. This visit takes place just after a Toddler Group class, during a time when the Nursery School children are outdoors and the child's future special teacher is available to meet with mother and child and introduce them in relative peace to the layout of the room and the toys. While the parents' and parent–child visits and related feelings are often mentioned in Toddler Group directly, every child brings his concerns indirectly in his behavior.

For many, now progressed to the developmental concerns around comparisons and competition, the main worry focuses on how they will show up, especially without their mothers' supportive presence. For others, the leaving of Toddler Group and prospective leaving of mother stirs anxiety over mixed love/hate feelings, about wishes and concerns as to who will get rid of whom, and with some, early qualms of conscience bring worries about being liked. Thus, fears, anger, and guilt may prompt children to view their future teachers and classmates as critical, punitive, and aggressive, and this conflicts with happy anticipation at growing bigger. We note these worries and the ways used to ward them off, and help the parents note them, too. We discuss some of them individually with parent and child, some with the whole group. We clarify the realities as best as possible, read books about nursery school, and point out similarities with Toddler Group activities. We assure the children and parents of our continuing interest in and relationship with them, our visits in the Nursery School, and their using the toddler room for some Nursery School activities. We work on anger and missing and the pleasure of growing up and away. During the last three weeks we use a paper chain with six links, to represent the six last classes and the six children in our group. After each class one child severs and takes home one link and we count the remaining ones. We bake cookies together to sweeten the last day, we have a take-home gift of a Toddler Group activity for each as a concrete souvenir, and we guess at the year's achievement by the way they leave us.

PART **II.**

What We Have Learned

CHAPTER 3

Self-Care and the Mother–Child Relationship

When we integrated and studied our data (E. Furman, 1992), we were at once impressed with evidence which confirmed our previous finding as to the important role of bodily self-care in the personality development of the toddler. At the same time, we were surprised by evidence of a reciprocal development in the mother, a change in her relationship with her child. The mother's ability to effect a shift from her earlier investment of him as a part of herself to a later investment of him as a separate, loved person was crucially linked to the child's success in achieving autonomy as an individual. And, although this mutual process concerns all aspects of the child's growing personality, it is especially focused on his body and its care. In order to clarify this, I shall first describe the pertinent aspects of the parent–child relationship and then the process of change and its vicissitudes around bodily care as they unfold during the toddler phase.

THE PARENT–CHILD RELATIONSHIP

For most, though by no means all people, having a baby

51

prompts a new developmental phase in their lives, that of becoming a parent in the emotional sense. This step into the
phase of parenthood (E. Furman, 1969a) is characterized by the
specific nature of the mother's and father's investment of their
child (i.e., their way of relating with him). They lovingly invest
their baby both as a part of themselves and as a separate person,
and at first their love of him stems predominantly from the
former rather than the latter aspect. There is, moreover, a
difference between a mother's and father's ways of investing
the infant as part of themselves. Whereas both parents relate
to their child as a mental part of themselves, the mother also
makes him a part of her body. This investment is continued
from the months of pregnancy—when the child really was a
part of her body—into the postnatal period when holding and
nursing come close to reconstituting their bodily unit. This
forms the basis of a mother's relationship to her baby. Biological
motherhood and breast-feeding facilitate but by no means
guarantee this development. Some adoptive mothers succeed
in investing their baby as a bodily part of themselves, some
biological mothers do not. I therefore speak of a mother as the
person who in caring for her infant cares for him as a mental
and bodily part of herself and, since a mother usually extends
to her baby the most positive aspects of her self-love, she treats
him as the most valuable part of herself. This is crucial in enabling her to keep him in mind at all times, to care for him
continuously even at the expense of her own comfort, fatigue,
and satisfaction of other interests, while sensing and meeting
his needs and stimulating his pleasure-seeking urges through
pleasurable contact with his body (fondling, holding, nursing,
cleansing). For the most part, this means that what is good for
the mother is good for the baby. For example, the nursing
mother usually relies on the sensations in her breasts to gauge
whether and when her baby is hungry while, at the same time,
her milk supply is regulated by the baby's nursing. In fact, the
bodily unit of mother and infant is reflected in the double
meaning of the very word *nursing* as it applies to mother's and
child's part. And when the baby is distressed or ill, mother feels
as responsible for putting it right as she would for regaining
her own well-being.

At the same time, a mother's investment in her baby as a separate person also needs to take place from the very start. This aspect of her relationship, the caring for and about him as another individual, enables her to learn his own ways and to respect them, assuring that her needs will not conflict with his; for example, that in fondling him as much as she wants, she does not overstep his tolerance for stimulation. In this way she facilitates his self-investment and in time helps him to own his body and functions.

With the child's growth, the balance between the two aspects of the relationship shifts to increase the love of the child as a person in his own right. The balance needs to remain flexible, however, so that at times when the older child regresses and again needs to be taken care of in a more infantile way, such as during illness, upset, or fatigue, mother's investment can shift back to an earlier balance in order to meet her child's needs at this given time. In spite of increasing their love of the child as a separate person during his growing up, and indeed throughout his life into adulthood, the parents' relationship with him retains a special and much greater aspect of self-love than any other relationship. The happiness and success or the distress and misfortune of the fully adult child forever affects the very core of his parents' selves.

The toddler phase is a period of drastic ongoing shift in the nature of the mother's relationship, from love of self to love of other. Since it is a back and forth development, often changing from hour to hour, it also demands enormous flexibility, a process that taxes a mother's capacity for change and resilience to its utmost.

OWNING ONE'S BODY AND TAKING CARE OF IT

The child's mastery of bodily self-care is the vehicle by which ownership of his body is transferred from mother to him. It is the fulcrum of change in the mother–child relationship, and it forms the basis for the child's growing concept of his bodily self. It characterizes the youngster who is "with it," who is "all there," neither whiny, clingy, and diffident, nor oppositional for opposition's sake. Mastery of self-care, more than any other single development, makes the toddler feel he is a person, a somebody.

The child's wish for "me do" and the zest he brings to putting it into practice is one of the hallmarks of being a toddler. "Me do" encompasses all areas of activity, be it turning on faucets, hammering, cooking, everything he sees his loved ones do, but for the most part the young toddler is content to imitate or to pretend. Not so when it concerns his own body, for in this area he wants to do for real, becomes very determined, and interferes with mother's ministrations if he does not get his own way.

> Cindy, 20 months old, sits next to her Mom at the table, enjoying her snack with all of us. She is still quite messy. Juice and cracker crumbs dribble down her chin. Mom reaches over and wipes the mess off Cindy's face. Cindy screams irritably. A few minutes later Mom repeats her wiping and Cindy repeats her screaming. Whereas some mothers would soon understand and find a way to work it out, Cindy's Mom either continues her wiping or, embarrassed by her daughter's screams, lets the mess dribble till the end of snack when the wiping is more of a job and Cindy screams longer and louder and has to be held by Mom lest she escape. After some days of this interaction, I, the teacher, suggest: "Maybe Cindy wants to be asked about wiping her face and then Cindy could tell Mom if she is ready for it." Mother looks surprised, then smiles looking at Cindy's beaming yes-nodding face. Soon we hear: "Cindy, are you ready to have me wipe your face? It'll feel better when it's clean." Cindy agrees, holds out her face for wiping and then surprises mother again with a gracious "Thank you." Both are pleased. All goes well when mother repeats her request, but of course she forgets occasionally and now Cindy responds with pulling away and yelling "No." Mother apologizes and promises to try harder. Cindy accepts her apology with dignity. After some days of this new, mutually respectful regime, Cindy fights for her next step in becoming Mommy to herself: she wants to do the wiping. Mother again has a hard time giving up, but this time I only need to say, "I think Cindy wants something more" and mother figures out that Cindy wants to do the wiping. She offers this to Cindy who agrees to the following compromise: Cindy will wipe herself and

Mom will help her by guiding her hand with the bigger cleanup at the end of the snack. Everyone is happy, and Cindy basks in her Mom's and the teacher's admiration for her new accomplishment.

Who owns the child's body, who gauges its needs, and who meets them are, for the toddler, the most crucial area of differentiating himself, of investing himself, and achieving bodily and mental self-esteem. He usually accomplishes this by internalizing mother's care of him and, step by step, learning to mother himself. He gauges his hunger and feeds himself; learns to know his sensations for eliminating and mastering toileting; dresses himself and cares for his clothes; learns to keep himself safe and avoid common dangers; is able to fall asleep on his own when tired. Although in Cindy's case, as in most others, the toddler's wish to take over his own care is manifestly signaled by impatience with or anger at mother's activity, by frustration at having to wait for her, or annoyance at the way she does it, the more important motivation for "me do" is the child's underlying admiration and love of what mother can do and resulting wish to become like her. In the context of a good-enough relationship, this admiring wish for identification also helps the child to prefer doing to being done for, to persevere with trying in spite of his frequent frustrating failures, and to tame his anger at mother, which inevitably accompanies the long process toward mastery. Usually, the more positive the relationship and the more consistent and enjoyable the mother's care has been, the sooner and more insistently does the child want to identify with her and do for himself.

For the mother this area is also the most crucial, and usually the most difficult, as she now has to make some of her owning of the child's body and bodily care available to him for his use and transform her relationship into one of loving his body and its care much more as his, much less as her own. Cindy, like most healthy toddlers, leads the way and alerts Mom that the next step is due. Mother is not as ready as Cindy but, with just a little additional help, begins to catch up. She shows that it goes against the grain by forgetting to ask Cindy's permission, and by needing a little help again with the next step, but she also shows her success in her efforts by apologizing for slipping up and by finding pleasure in Cindy's achievement, and sharing Cindy's enjoyment of it.

THE SHARED STEPS IN ACHIEVING BODILY MASTERY

Sometimes the steps in the toddler doing for himself are minis-cule, sometimes huge. They do, however, group themselves into four successive stages on the way toward full mastery, or internalization, and each stage requires its own characteristic interaction with mother: (1) There is the "doing for" stage, with mother doing the caring for the child who essentially enjoys being done for. Already during babyhood this is never a pure stage; even then most mothers respect and accommodate to some aspects of the child's active participation. (2) Next comes the "doing with" stage, where mother and child, in varying proportion, share in the tasks, for example, proceeding from the child holding up his arms to assist with getting off his shirt to the child perhaps putting on his own jacket with mother pulling out the collar and starting the zipper. (3) Then comes the "standing by to admire" stage, where the child is doing some aspects of self-care without any assistance—maybe using spoon and fork for eating, or protecting himself by carefully staying out of the way of a moving swing. Mother is very much needed still to stand by, fully invested, to appreciate her child's efforts and achievement, and to support and share his pride in it. (4) The final stage is "doing for oneself," where the child has internalized both the mothering of himself and the satisfaction it brings to such an extent that mother's bodily presence and emotional investment are no longer necessary. Whatever the achievement is, that aspect of his body, its needs, and care are now owned by the child and provide him with a sense of well-being and self-esteem, his feeling good about himself as a person.

Just as the first "doing for" stage already involves some "doing with" and long precedes toddlerhood in the bodily area, so the third stage of "standing by to admire," and especially the fourth one of really "doing for oneself" extend well beyond toddlerhood. But the important basics are best accomplished during this phase to enable the child to cope with the developmental tasks of the subsequent preschool phase. This phase includes the integration of concerns about sexual differences and the child's place vis-à-vis the parents' husband–wife relationship; the ability to adjust in a nursery school where he has to relate with a teacher who is not a mere mother substitute, and where his investment in activities and play presupposes a considerable degree of independent mastery of bodily needs.

The child's success in getting to own his body and meet its needs depends throughout on his mother's ability to stay "in tune." Most mothers miss the toddler's first signals of readiness for "me do" and need his persistent help, usually in the form of protest and uncooperativeness, to help them along in their task of surrendering ownership and shifting their self-love of it to love of his owning and doing. Most mothers find it especially puzzling and even exasperating at times to follow the zigzag line of the child's progress—protesting often, welcoming mother's taking over at other times, or even refusing to do for himself on some days the very self-care he had previously so proudly achieved. The best first signs of a mother's appropriately balanced investment and potential flexibility are the child's signals, and especially his persistence in signaling. It means he senses and trusts that she can respond to him, and she usually does. Even when, as with Cindy's mother, she seemed to need additional help from someone who could feel with both of them, the fact that mother can readily use this help and that the child has not given up signaling suggest that mother is fairly ready to do her part. We find that many mothers are able to use additional help to effect the necessary change, even when their interaction with the child has been at a standstill for some time.

When 22-month-old Jane's mother first arrived she asked where the changing table was. I explained that we did not have one, that we had learned that most toddlers like so much to stand on their own feet and take an active part in everything, and that therefore mothers work it out with their youngsters in this way in the adjacent private bathroom. Mother shook her head in disbelief and with some irritation but, when the time came, she and Jane did work it out. Jane emerged from the bathroom beaming, mother somewhat harassed. After a while we heard they had discontinued the being "done for" stage at home too, with Jane eager to dump and flush the diaper contents, pulling her own pants off and back on, even talking about using the toilet. Mother then added reflectively, "Getting her changed used to be such a struggle. I thought her standing up would be even worse, but it's really much easier now. I guess she was ready."

Such capacity for mother and toddler to get back in tune testifies not only to the health of their relationship but to the fact that help is most readily integrated when mother and child are still in the process of tackling this developmental task. But progressive steps are not always so easily taken. Sometimes a mother does recognize the child's wish for "me do," but begrudges it, and can't allow herself to enjoy it.

John's mother dressed her nearly 2-year-old in her lap, with him struggling and kicking and her alternating desperate pleas of "But you need to help me" with strangleholds as she pulled on his snowpants or jacket. Finally she would stand him up and say angrily, "Well, you can just do it yourself. I am through!" John would then, with equal anger, push and pull at his garments, give up in frustration, and have a temper tantrum, or run around teasingly, or helplessly surrender to mother's renewed dressing efforts. When he did manage to get on his jacket, he looked more defiant and sheepish than proud.

Jeremy, just under 2, simply let himself be dressed, cuddling into his Mom. He either had never shown initiative or had long ceased to do so. Although a smart and capable boy, Jeremy sensed correctly that, with him as with his older siblings, mother especially enjoyed their bodily care and was very reluctant to surrender it. At the same time, mother's rather frequent absences and unavailability already posed a threat (he got very upset and angry at good-bye times) and perhaps made him reluctant, as it were, to leave her. Adapting to mother's need, he appeared to have surrendered his potential independence for the sake of keeping her infantile love—but at a cost. He would cast sidelong glances at his happy, accomplished peers and then look down as if shamed, and he often refused to attempt new activities, insisting on mother's help, never trusting himself to master anything. By pointing this out to them, mother and child could be helped to recognize Jeremy's wish to do for himself and to do well, and then they took the first steps in working on Jeremy's dressing together and building his self-esteem with each proud achievement.

The "doing with" stage, once embarked upon, is often a satisfying period for mother and child, but can also reach a plateau or turn into an increasingly unhelpful interaction. With toileting, for example, it often shows in mother continuing to wipe her child's behind ("He can's get it really clean"). The child then not only never fully takes charge of his body but also continues to experience a passive stimulation. Although this kind of getting stuck may be caused by many factors in mother and child, a significant one is the reluctance to face the next step. "Standing by to admire" is perhaps the hardest step of all for the mother, the time when she feels not needed, the time when she truly has to surrender her direct involvement with the child's body without withdrawing from him. It is the very time when the child needs her most to love him in a new way. Without it, his achievement has no value and cannot be internalized in a lastingly adaptive, satisfying way. Some mothers actually walk away to busy themselves with something else (most often with their own body—doing their nails, combing their hair, going to the bathroom). Some stand by, but their mind is not with the child. Some say, "I am so proud of you," as though the child's achievement were still theirs, instead of: "You really are doing a good job, how proud you can feel with yourself." Some show their persisting self-love in action.

Ellen's mother always had to improve her daughter's achievement, in fact making it her own. She did this not only with Ellen's body, such as adjusting her clothes and adding decorative items, but also with Ellen's activities, such as adding items to her picture to make it look better or fitting in some of the pieces of Ellen's puzzle. Mother's pride in the final result was matched by Ellen's dissatisfaction and often led to her actually destroying the product because it had become mother's, Ellen's own part seeming inadequate.

Even skilled achievements are joyless and unstable when they lack mother's loving investment.

Jennifer's mother very much wanted to do the right thing and decided to set the pace by expecting her 2-year-old to dress herself. Jennifer had the necessary skills at her disposal, but neither she nor mother truly enjoyed either the process or the achievement. Soon Jennifer made a teasing frustrating struggle out of it, dawdling or running around, or acting helpless until considerations of time often forced mother either to sit it out with constant firm exhortations or to end up dressing Jennifer. The little girl felt she was losing rather than gaining something by dressing herself. Mother's expectation reflected her investment of Jennifer as a part of herself, and was not accompanied by a change to caring about her as a separate person. I commented to mother and child, "It looks a bit like Jennifer has to make such a big fuss to have Mommy close. Perhaps she feels that if you dress yourself you miss out on a loving time with Mommy." Jennifer understood at once. Mother needed time to work this out for herself in her weekly meetings with their therapist, but, to start with, even some extra hugs with dressing helped.

Regardless of whether a child actually knows how to take care for his body, unless his admiring loving of mother's care motivated him to learn her skills, and unless they are internalized with mother's appropriate appreciation and love of them as his own, they will not reach the last phase of "doing for oneself" in a reliable manner. Instead, they tend to remain subject to regression and/or do not add to the child's good feeling about himself. Lack of self-worth in bodily mastery tends to carry over to unstable mental self-esteem and remains, as our follow-up indicates, a sign of this toddler's development having gone awry. We have seen this occur not only in instances where the child learns to care for himself out of defiance of or compliance with mother. It is strikingly evident in cases where the child has learned aspects of self-care, such as dressing, from temporary caretakers (as in day care), or from siblings or peers, or even from the father. We have seen it also in instances where the child's self-care resulted from missing mother or her care and was accomplished during periods of mother's unavailability. When the child bypasses the step of, "I want to mother myself as mother does," and when the transfer of mother's love to loving investment of self-care does not accompany his accomplishment, it does not contribute to his self-esteem or loving self-regard. It may also adversely affect the mother's feelings for her child and pose an obstacle to her appropriate investment in him, even if, at one level, she is glad not to be needed. With some mother–child relationships, such leaving out or diminished use of the mother in acquiring self-care, appears to result from actual deficits in maternal investment and/or excessive unavailability. The child's accomplishment then suggests that he came to mother himself in order to ward off his missing of her love rather than by internalizing her love, and it therefore fails to serve as a source of self-love. This did not apply to the mothers of our toddlers. With them, our observations suggest that a mother's relative failure in effecting the necessary shifts in investment were often related to a marked admixture of negative feelings. The negative aspect of the mother's investment was either part of her self-investment (e.g., her own lack of self-esteem as a mother extended to the child) or part of the considerable admixture of aggression in her investment of the child as a separate person. The former is, for example, evident in the vignette of Ellen, whose mother always needed to improve her child's accomplishment and, in doing so, conveyed that anything Ellen did would not be good enough. The latter difficulty often shows in a mother's denial of her child's signals ("Oh, I don't think he's ready for that yet"), but she may then become very angry at her child when they finally work on mastery and the child does not perform well. In such instances, as in the case of Mary below, the mother's continued investment of the child as a part of herself protects the child from the anger mother would experience toward her if she viewed her as separate.

Mary's mother diapered her in a prone position until she was 2 years old, claiming that Mary was not ready to use the potty. Mother realized that she especially liked the infantile bodily relationship with her children and Mary wisely adapted to this and submitted without complaint. But when, in part as a result of other progressive steps during Toddler Group, Mary finally asserted herself and mother embarked with her on the "doing with" stage, all loving patience left her in spite of her good intentions. She repeatedly burst out with harsh anger at Mary's incidents of wetting and soiling, much to her own chagrin. This difficulty with anger was part of all of mother's relationships, but had not manifested itself with Mary as long as mother owned Mary's body.

"I DID NOT EXPECT IT OF HIM"

A mother's attitude or verbalization of "I did not expect it of him" often encapsulates the essence of her investment of him as a part of herself. It implies that the child's growth proceeds via mother's rather than the child's readiness, and often applies not only to matters of bodily ownership and care but extends to many other areas of his personality. On the one hand it reflects her sense of total responsibility, which is so crucial to her continuous care of him, and which, when something is wrong with her child, not only makes her feel guilty but fuels her efforts to put it right again. It is the very feeling we count on, for example, to help a mother initiate and support her child's treatment for bodily or emotional illness. On the other hand, however, and with her toddler especially, this attitude typically leads a mother to assume that she, and only she, is the cause of whatever the child feels and does, disregarding feelings and conflicts that stem from within the child or from experiences which were relatively unrelated to the mother.

Tim, close to 2, did not know how to peddle a tricycle or climb up our small slide. Large motor skills were not his forte but the striking thing was that he refused to practice, although he longingly watched his peers, some better than he at it, some not. His Mom told us she felt this was all due to the fact that her earlier illness had prevented her from doing these activities with him enough and she resolved to make up for it. She and Tim had many good outdoor activity times near their home where Tim worked on these skills quite happily and he also did so in our playground when he was out there first or last. But the moment the other toddlers were around doing the same activities, Tim gave up and refused to use the equipment. Mom practiced ever more with him, and each time reported how good Tim was getting with his tricycle. She could not understand, sometimes puzzling, sometimes rationalizing, why he refused at certain times. It was quite evident to us that Tim felt inferior in the face of competition and our other observations as well as reports from home indicated that Tim's feeling derived from him comparing himself with his older brothers and father. It took much tactful work to help Mom appreciate that she could not help Tim by merely investing his motor control more lovingly but needed to assist him in facing and coping with his helpless envy of the bigger males in the family.

Holly, 26 months old, had waited with her mother in the toddler room before the start of class and had, with mother's permission, played with puzzles from the teachers' drawers. When we arrived and brought out these puzzles, Holly became furious at me, yelled at and attacked me, while at the same time backing away as though I would go after her. I told her it looked like she expected me to be very angry at her, which I was not, but perhaps she felt bad about something. The story of her use of the puzzles was then blurted out and Holly indeed was very guilty. We agreed that she need not feel so bad because the puzzles were not damaged, but that she would feel better if next time she would wait to ask teacher's okay before helping herself. Then we would plan ahead just what she could play with. Mother noticed how guilty Holly felt but was flabberghasted, "How could she feel guilty when I did not tell her it was bad?" In this as in other instances, mother had altogether disregarded her little girl's own feelings and conflicts, and hence been unable to empathize and help her.

Some mothers disregard not only feelings and conflicts but their child's personality functions. They may talk about him in his presence and claim he did not hear or know what they were saying because "I did not tell him," as though his perceptions and knowledge functioned only with what she selected for him. Or they may talk for him and answer questions directed to him as though his speech was really theirs, or urge him to tell the teachers specific events of their choosing about home experiences. They are then quite nonplussed and embarrassed when the child refuses to comply or, worse, tells what was meaningful to him. Thus Peter told us that at the zoo Dad told him to pee on a bush, and Bart failed to repeat mother's nice account of going to a children's theater and blurted out instead that he tweeked a woman's nose because she came too close and touched his face. Less humorously, mothers frequently feel that they need to order and control a child's every move, be it in play, activities, or self-care, never crediting the child with remembering, knowing, having ideas of his own, or really wanting to do things well. And if he does make a mistake, they take it as proof of his inability to master for himself instead of sympathizing with the child's feelings of failure and assuring him that he can put it right and will soon learn to do it well.

Of course, the mothers who disclaim their responsibility and quickly put the blame for the child's difficulty on others are not feeling less but more guilty, hence the need for warding it off.

Alan's mother blamed his hitting on his older brother's mistreatment of him, but this only thinly and temporarily veiled her guilt about her own loss of temper and for not protecting Alan from the brother. Actually Alan's physical aggression also stemmed from other sources beyond mother's control but she could not consider these for some time.

In describing the effects of mothers' investment of the child as parts of themselves I do not wish, as the mothers do, to disregard the child's contribution to their interactions. Toddlers' individual personalities, conflicts, and experiences may delay or interfere with phase-appropriate development in such a way that they do not signal their readiness for progressive steps or misuse their mothers' willingness to own them for defensive purposes.

Bess, a 2-year-old with a very well-structured personality, had herself a rough day in Toddler Group. She was irritable and unable to settle down to activities. At the end of it she shouted at mother: "I am very angry at you, you are a bad Mommy," which mother accepted, attributing it to that morning's argument between them. When I suggested that I did not know about Mommy being so bad, but perhaps Bess was pretty angry at Bess for having had a hard day, Bess suddenly looked guilty and, with great seriousness, agreed, much to mother's surprise. Bess often used this defense to ward off inner conflict and found a willing partner in mother.

Sally, already past 2 years old, still wanted mother to diaper her. Sometimes she even wanted her diapers changed when they were dry, which mother attributed to Sally not being ready to use the toilet and not knowing when diapers were really wet. But Sally, it turned out, wanted mother, over and over again, to put on her, Sally's bottom something else that was an appendage, hence the insistent demand for a ministration that never turned out satisfactory for long. She wanted mother to make her into a boy, and her demand for ever new diapers warded off this wish and expectation from mother.

A toddler's lack of zest for self-care and demands for or acquiescence in being done for quite often obscure low self-esteem and harsh early guilt, and find alternate or defensive gratification in mother's infantile investment of him. Yet in each of these cases, the child's feelings of inferiority and his or her turning anger against the self also grew out of mother not having responded to the child's readiness. She had not helped the child gain self-esteem through loving internalization of her love, and had failed to channel his aggression into purposeful activity in the process. Without this early self-esteem and well-directed energy, children easily feel incapable of coping with concerns about their bodies being sexually adequate, just as they then often feel inadequate in attempting skills and activities. They fall back on mother doing for them as a solution to their difficulties.

Perhaps the most unhelpful way in which a parent's self-investment of the child may manifest itself is the use, or rather misuse, of him for the parent's erotic or aggressive gratification. We illustrated this, at the start of this chapter, when we mentioned parents fondling their child for pleasure but without regard for his tolerance for stimuli. Tickling, bouncing him up and down, kissing him sensuously, or exposing him to parental nudity, toileting, or sexual activity are other forms, especially when the parents either fail to notice or actually prohibit or punish the child's response, or deny there even is a response. Alternately, a mother may not limit her toddler's inappropriate sexual behavior, such as intruding on others' bathrooming, exposing their genitals to others, or masturbating in front of them during, say, storytime in a group. She seems unaware, at these times, not only of the reaction of other children, but of the fact that her own child has feelings and ends up either overstimulated or conflicted or both. Likewise, with aggression, mothers may fail to limit their child's aggression or be unaware of the child's feelings about mother's aggression. Although fathers are sometimes the main initiators in these interactions, the mother's compliance and failure to feel with and protect her child points to her share in it.

The various manifestations of a mother's no longer phase-appropriate relationship with her toddler are of course widely encountered in her relationship with her much older or even adult children, as are the devastating effects on the child's personality. At later stages such interactions have become complex, tend to be rigidly fixed, and are hard to change. During the toddler phase, by contrast, a mother's relative shifts in her relationship with her child are a part of a phase-appropriate developmental task in her mothering and hence generally still quite flexible. Even when there have been delays or when the child's conflicts have complicated matters, limited assistance from the therapist and/or teacher is mostly well utilized. As long as the helper is able to feel with and respect mother and child and, instead of getting between them or posing as the better mother, assists them to reestablish communication, mother and child tend to appreciate the intervention—perhaps because getting in tune gives so much satisfaction to both. We find that a mother who gets in tune in this phase is likely to remain in tune in subsequent phases. Even a very partial success, however, is well worth achieving. So is a mother's ability to acknowledge her difficulty to her child, apologize for it, and encourage him to alert her when it recurs (as was the case with Cindy's mother who kept wiping her little girl's face). Even when a mother cannot consistently alter her behavior, attributing the blame to herself frees the child from undue guilt over his wish for independence, and enables him to feel good about his efforts.

Ultimately, being loved only as a part of a parent means not being loved, being unacceptable as oneself. The lasting personality adaptations to such a state vary enormously and may encompass the most severe pathologies, but basically they are a means of coping with a lack of positive investment in one's real self.

CHAPTER 4

Fathers

Our implicit attitude of valuing and respecting the father's role in the family (chapters 1, 2) derives from an understanding gained over years of experience in observing and working with children of all ages and their parents at our Center and School (R. A. Furman, 1983; E. Furman, 1987; E. Furman and R. A. Furman, 1989). Here I shall only briefly summarize some of this basic thinking as it applies to the child up to about 3 years (i.e., from birth through infancy, toddlerhood, and the beginning of the preschool phase).

We have stressed the great importance of the father as the protector of the mother–baby couple and supporter of the mother's mothering during the most vulnerable early months. This support and protection enables her to devote herself to her baby, to integrate (and reintegrate) motherhood into her personality, and, despite its hardships and frustrations, to learn to experience it as a valuable and valued aspect of herself. This initial paternal role, so crucial for the mother and hence the baby, is a difficult one for many fathers, in part because neither they nor others truly appreciate its value to mother and child. It is also because fathers and others, confronted with the exquisite twosome of mother–baby interaction, forget about the essence of the family as a threesome. This essence is there from conception, but its interdependent relationships change dramatically with the changing developmental needs of all its partners, especially those of the growing child. There is a tendency for everyone, and fathers especially, to feel that two is company and three is a crowd, that he can only participate by being either the baby or the mother. The extent to which both parents can value father as protector and supporter, make room for him, accord him his rightful and necessary place, will help him to meet his responsibilities. It will also determine whether his bodily care of the baby—and this is not an essential part of his role—is undertaken to assist the mother and/or to understand and appreciate better her role with their baby, or whether it represents a way of intruding into the mother–infant unit, of replacing the mother or being a "better" mother. Once she has established herself in her mothering role, once the baby has begun to settle into his rhythm of living and growing, and the family has coalesced around him, the father can, if he is so inclined, make an excellent baby-sitter. More importantly though, he becomes the main "additional person." In this capacity he does not substitute for the mother but builds a new and different relationship with the infant, one not focused on need-fulfillment but on simple play and activities which form the special bond between them. Now mother participates as supporter and protector. She remains available in case of need, protects their twosome, and shares in their enjoyment without intruding unless the game gets too boisterous, and mother, knowing that too much fun will result in an aftermath of upset, intercedes.

In this way the father starts off on his important role of bringing the child to the world, to new sensations and experiences, while the mother tends to bring the world to the child, carefully screening and gauging it to his comfort. As the infant grows into a young toddler, as his bodily needs are less urgent and constant, and he begins even to meet them himself a bit, there is more time and energy available to go off and explore Dad's world with him, within and without the home, to draw on his power and know-how, and to give and get some respite from the intense love–hate and body-centered tug-of-war in the relationship with the mother. The father's role with the mother is most important during the toddler phase. In order to weather the "seduction" of the child's impulses to hurt and mess and the stressful realignment in her investment of him, as well as in order to remain consistently available to help him tame his anger for the sake of their mutual love, she not only needs occasional respites and appreciation of her mothering, but also opportunities to reconstitute herself as an adult. Occasions like a truly civilized late dinner with father can do wonders, as do the times when he sympathetically hears her out about the hardships of the day. Once again, father's actual caring for their toddler may be a help or a hindrance, depending on the feelings that prompt it and go with it. And this, as we have had opportunity to observe, will affect mother, father, and child. It may serve to build a harmonious threesome or exacerbate tensions and burden their relationships and development.

In working with over one hundred children who grew up in single-parent families through bereavement, divorce, or other circumstances, we have become acutely aware of the importance of both parents and their relationship with each other for their children (E. Furman and R. A. Furman, 1989). The diminishment and hurt to the self of having only one parent were deeply felt by older toddlers, as was the lack of opportunity for loving and being loved by two parents which caused an unhappy excess of negative over positive feelings.

We have also worked with several fathers who were their very young children's primary caretakers. None of them had originally planned on taking this role, but they assumed it willingly and with full dedication when circumstances, such as the mother's sudden death or illness, presented this opportunity or need. In some of these cases the family's financial situation made it unnecessary for the father to earn a living, and he could be available around the clock. Despite their loving devoted care, these fathers did not invest the child as a bodily part of themselves, even when it was a baby, and they needed more regular time for themselves and away from the child than the usual good-enough mother. Eventually they used extensive substitute care from housekeepers or grandmothers. Various reasons were given, but one father insightfully described his ongoing infant care as a threat to his adult personality, not just to his masculinity. Although he used the therapist and close relatives much as a mother usually uses the father, he needed time off "to put myself together, to do my own things so as to be myself." Apart from many other implications of this, the lack of a bodily unit between father and child makes for a very different parent–child interplay during toddlerhood when the child takes over the bodily care from him. However, the fact that the fathers we have worked with did not invest their children as a bodily part of themselves, does not imply that they did not invest the child's body and needs. Often they responded intensely, with indulgence or prohibition, to the impulse manifestations which, in the very young child, are usually associated with need-fulfillment, be it greed, messing, or hurting. Also, like the mothers and from the beginning, they responded to the child's maleness and femaleness, as part of self and as other, and stimulated the child's reciprocal response, even when they kept themselves and their bodily functions private and did not unduly stimulate the child's body while caring for it.

"I NEED MY DADDY"

Although we were well aware of the toddler's deep hurt to the self caused by a father's absence from the home, we were impressed by the extent to which the little boys and girls in our Toddler Group derived self-gratification from just having a father, from being able to show him to others as their father, and from being able to elicit and focus his attention on themselves. Each year, as soon as we talked about being ready to invite fathers and the monthly Visitors Schedule was available for sign-up, the children pleaded at school and at home for their Dad to come, to come sooner and to stay longer than anyone else's Dad, and they happily anticipated the day. And when he was a nice, important, wonderful, big man in everyone's eyes as much as in their own, they felt more worthwhile as girls or as boys, really just more worthwhile. Regardless of how satisfactory the visit turned out to be, they proudly referred back to it, always wanted him to come again, and enviously missed him when another Dad visited.

When a father took a long time to schedule a visit, perhaps because he found it hard to get away from work, did not consider a visit so important, or was reluctant for other reasons, there were insistent complaints, angry impatience, and manifest envy during other fathers' visits, until at last mother and child prevailed upon him. But for the children who really did not have their father in the home the hurt was so severe that they said nothing, as if needing to hide a shameful defect. They never mentioned their fathers and never joined in others' talk about them. During fathers' visits they muttered a polite affectless hello when introduced, bent their heads low over whatever they busied themselves with, and stayed just a little closer to their mothers. Had it not been for their subdued demeanor and occasional furtive, longing side glances, it could have seemed that they paid no attention, ignored, or even denied the existence of fathers. Some mothers, like Carole's (see chapter 8), were at first unaware of their children's pain. Others sensed it and tried in vain to compensate with extra loving attention, but did not dare or know how to broach the topic with them.

Debbie had not seen her father since she was a baby. He had even then not been close to her, was periodically mentally incapacitated, and resided in a distant part of the country. The therapist and teachers had early on confirmed the mother's vague feeling that his unavailability chagrined Debbie and made her feel deprived. Mother was helped to empathize with Debbie in words. They began to send him letters, and Debbie spontaneously made pictures to enclose for him. Even before he responded, mother's understanding and support of Debbie's active attempts to engage him with her gifts helped the little girl. She proudly announced that she was making a painting for her Dad, and saved her best productions for him. She began to acknowledge her longing for him when other fathers visited, and participated animatedly when we helped her explain to the group that she did have a Daddy but he could not come because he lived far away and was sometimes ill. When a gift from him finally arrived, she showed it off with almost speechless happiness. She seemed suddenly taller and more zestful, chattered away, showed off her skills, and joined happily in conversations at snack with an air of, "I am a somebody. I have things to say."

Toward the end of the school year, father's impending visit was announced. Everyone quietly shared Debbie's mixture of happy and apprehensive anticipation during this generally ambivalent period of working on Father's Day gifts. He stayed for several days and came to Toddler Group just before leaving town. As already reported by mother, we saw him relate to Debbie as if she still were the baby he had known, carrying her on his shoulders, trying to feed her, and help her with her jacket. He was quiet and gentle and Debbie equally quietly and gently helped him see her as the competent older toddler she was, demonstrating her self-care, engaging him in a table game, showing off her school, and all she could do in it. He marveled at her appreciatively, said how lucky she was, and how happy it made him that he could see her being so nice in her nice school. They had a few tender minutes alone together on the playground while the rest of us prepared for going home. When she joined us she had her arms around him and he cried with feeling. Debbie indeed had a Daddy. The children were awed, and mothers and teachers had tears in their eyes.

Much mother–child talk followed this experience and many painful facts had to be integrated, but for Debbie, father's visit made all the difference. He had not just become available as a boost for her self-regard but as a real person to relate with. The next time when our snack was the same as during his visit, she cried bitterly, accepted mother's and our sympathy with her missing of him, and then ate heartily as she happily reminisced with us.

During the following three years there were many ups and downs in the father–child contact, but Debbie never lost her inner relationship with him. This helped her capacity to feel and her self-esteem. It also paved the way for her to experience the family as a threesome and to accept her place in it.

Debbie had a loving nearby grandfather, uncle, and older cousin, all of whom served her as father substitutes and were willing to visit Toddler Group in that capacity. For Debbie, however, as for all other children we have worked with, they were simply substitutes—better than nothing but very different from the "real" father. Knowing how hard it is to alleviate this hurt, we have tried hard to work toward reestablishing contact with fathers, and short of loss through death, have mostly succeeded, even in seemingly hopeless circumstances.

However, even an available father may not meet his child's need for self-enhancement. We became aware that the youngsters who most insistently demanded their father's visit, most eagerly anticipated it, and most often proudly referred back to it were most unsure of his interest in and affection for them. The actual visits tended to be disappointing, exacerbating the children's anger and lack of self-worth, and sometimes prompted idealization during his absence to ward off recognition of the disappointment.

> When 22-month-old Jeanie's long awaited Daddy finally came, she did everything to engage him. She had put on a special dress, she had a book ready for him to read to her, she showed him her favorite toys. In part prompted by mother, he did his best, but his attention wandered, he missed what Jeanie said to him, yawned, and pretty soon he walked over to the bookshelf and got absorbed in reading on his own. Jeanie pathetically tried to reengage him, first by flirting with him, then by excitedly teasing him—approaches she knew sometimes worked with him at home—but she never managed to hold his full interest for more than a few minutes, even when he stayed close by. Snack proved more successful as she served him and made a point of sharing their favorite crackers. Later father was more able to participate with her in an activity when the teacher joined them too, but Jeanie was not fooled. Her happy sparkle was defensive and, after a boisterously affectionate good-bye, she was subdued and avoided looking at us. Father had liked her dress, her excitement, and her serving of food, but not her.

In similar circumstances other children tried to boss their father, or tried to keep him captive by isolating him from mother and everyone else, or could not bear to have him leave, overcome with angry frustration when their hopes had not materialized. Sometimes they then vented their anger on mother afterwards and/or regressed in impulse control and ability to engage in activities.

For some children, the father's visit occasioned a different humiliation. They were ashamed of his behavior. To demonstrate his perfection was as important as to be able to count on his loving attention. One boy who struggled a great deal with his own excited and aggressive eating impulses, was deeply ashamed of his father's "greedy" eating, and quietly reprimanded him for taking too many cookies at one time. He was only partly relieved when we pointed out that Dad could not know our rules and when Dad apologized. They also watched for their father's least transgression in thoughtfulness and politeness to others, looked ashamed when they thought he had not acted right, and often looked to us to make sure we did not disapprove.

John's father, by contrast, spontaneously thanked our cook, when he accompanied his boy to the kitchen to get the snack cart. Nothing could have made his son more proud and pleased than our appreciation of his father's kindness, although, just minutes earlier, John had tried to "one-up" his Dad by not sharing his blocks with him and by building the tallest tower, the first of its kind for this youngster.

The father's self-enhancing value to the toddler is strictly limited to his availability in addition to the mother. The moment he accompanied his child to Toddler Group instead of her, he was second best in his own child's eyes and, instead of arousing envy in the other children, posed something of a threat to them, an "I hope that doesn't happen to me." Not having a mother is, at this age, much worse than not having a father. This applied as much to a half-hour's substituting while mother was on a special errand as to a month when mother was ill or had a new baby. The children's response in these situations often came as a painful surprise to the mothers and especially fathers. In spite of the therapists and teachers alerting them beforehand that the child might miss his mother, some parents expected the occasion to be a special treat and tried to prepare their child in these terms. Some mothers did not believe they would really be missed, pointed out that the father is used to caring for their child, that the child always wants to see more of Dad, or never objects to father taking over, or that it will give father a special chance to relate and perhaps at least show him just what mother is up against all the time. The fathers, for their part, often did see it as a special chance, looked forward to it, and in most instances, mothered their youngsters very well, often proving themselves better in this capacity than they had been as visiting fathers. They were therefore quite chagrined to see, or to be alerted to, their toddler's direct and indirect manifestations of feeling deprived and of missing their mothers.

The youngsters' upset showed most clearly at times of bodily need-fulfillment, dressing, eating, getting hurt, toileting. The very ones who, during father's earlier visit, sometimes provocatively insisted that he help with their jacket or take them to the bathroom or help them with snack, now sadly would not eat, cried for mother when hurt, wet themselves repeatedly, or ran around wildly, refusing to dress or be dressed, and in the end had a tantrum followed by heartfelt sobs. Others, by contrast, all of a sudden quietly cared for themselves with more effort and success than they had ever shown with their mothers. One might have thought this resulted from their fathers' more helpful, usually more matter-of-fact attitude, except that these skills brought the children no pleasure and disappeared as soon as mother was back. Moreover, these youngsters showed other sudden and transitory signs of identification with the absent mother, such as sitting just like her, doing an activity the way she would, or, when mother was with a new baby, caring for the doll as a baby, play otherwise never engaged in before or after mother's absence.

When we helped father and child to recognize the missing of mother, when the father could overcome his hurt ("But she has *me*. Why would she miss mother?" questioned one father), could empathize with his child and address the feelings in words, the child's behavioral manifestations subsided and they forged a new, meaningful bond between them, one born of feeling and being felt with, of understanding and being understood. The fathers could then acknowledge to their child what they did not know, and the child willingly told them just how Mommy did this or that. Both could also allow us to help them make things for Mommy to take home for her, to talk about what she was doing right now, or used to do and would do again in Toddler Group. They could be helped to prepare for all they would share with Mom at home, so she would know and not miss out altogether. For many fathers these experiences were most meaningful, altered their attitude to family togetherness, and helped them toward a better understanding of their child in many respects. One father in particular remained very alert to his son's need of his mother, spotted his missing of her during a later part of the year when the mother had partly withdrawn, and helped her to resume her maternal functioning.

One boy needed his father in a different way for self-protection.

During a period when Kevin's mother was especially upset and at times angry and scary, he not only wanted his Dad but helped himself by calling him up on our toy phone. Unfortunately, in a later phase of development, when Kevin's own angry competition with father was prominent, he cast his Dad in the mold of the earlier angry punitive mother, and became afraid of him as well as of other men.

"MY DAD IS A MAN"

The toddlers' relating to their fathers as a part of themselves is, of course, inseparable from his importance as a separate loved person. Both aspects of the relationship with him found expression in those interactions which showed their awareness of his masculinity. This does not necessarily imply knowledge of his genitals and their functions or of sexual differences, a topic to be taken up later (see chapter 5). Rather, what is involved is a much less explicit sense of him as a man, defined for the child by his special overall bodily characteristics, attitudes, pursuits, role in the family, ways of relating to each of its members, and expectation of the child's response to him. To have his manliness, to draw on all it represents for one's own self-regard, was important for boys and girls and codetermined their interactions with him as a person.

The boys stressed father's bigness and work and leaned on it to aggrandize themselves, sometimes by extolling these virtues in words, sometimes by wanting and showing off manly possessions (real or in toy form), and often by imitating him. Boys would eat a lot like Daddy, want the biggest cookie, or use the workbench like Daddy. During the fathers' visits, however, the boys' mixed feelings about him as a separate person showed as well, and sometimes the fathers' showed too.

> Max had often talked of father's tools, had in fact appropriated some of them occasionally at home and, in Toddler Group, proudly imitated Dad's mechanical skills at the workbench. When his father came, Max started to show this off to Dad in an "And now it's your turn to admire me" fashion, but Dad quickly took over and, much to Max's chagrin, did the showing off at the workbench himself. Mother sat by uneasily, but did not know how to help, so I asked Max whether he had given Dad his toy to use. Max shook his head "no," father caught on, and asked Max if he could borrow it, and Max then consented, recouping some of his dignity.

Some boys, like John in the earlier example, simply refused to share with their fathers, and some were very nice with them but displaced their feelings to visiting male therapists. Lionel, for example, was obviously displeased when these men visited, muttered "Not him again," and refused to do what he considered manly things, such as building a tall tower, while they were present, for fear of not showing up well.

The girls appropriated father's manliness in a different way. Although they too built tall towers and practiced at the workbench, these and similar activities were not used for this purpose. Above all, they wanted his exclusive attention, his loving admiration of themselves and of all they could do, and his bodily closeness. They talked about and showed off the things father liked about them and had given them, especially clothes, accessories, and jewelry which made them look pretty in his eyes. His bigness and type of work did not matter. During fathers' visits, they tried to command his full appreciative attention and, like Jeanie in the earlier example, did whatever they knew would work best with him to achieve it. This included being clever, showing off dancing or "gymnastics," flirting, snuggling excitedly into his lap, or teasing provocation. As with the boys, visits also highlighted the girls' aggression. Sometimes this showed in their possessively aggressive hugs or their hard pushes at his crotch while sitting on his lap. Sometimes they were bossy, controlling, and demanding, or their excitement deteriorated into aggressive misbehavior. And sometimes they held back, coyly or standoffishly, and drew closer to mother. Like the boys, the girls too responded to the visiting male therapists either by approaching them as they did their fathers or by showing some aspects of their feelings about their fathers.

A few fathers could enjoy their toddlers as the little persons they were and play and interact with them in a considerate, calm manner. Some were excited with their girls and inviting of the child's excited response, some were show-offy and competitive in various ways with the boys. A few were stiff and uncomfortable and had trouble engaging in activities with their sons or daughter. Instead of warmth they showed strictness and expected too much behavioral control or intellectual achievement. Although at first we thought that these fathers' discomfort was due to their concern about the unfamiliar setting, treatment-via-the-parent revealed that these fathers too tended to be excited and exciting with their toddlers and alternated this behavior with a defensive struggle against their impulses. Regardless of whether the fathers' excitement was overt or warded off, most of them had been active in taking care of their children's bodily needs, but this had not helped them to build a nonbodily, gratifying relationship with them.

MOTHER-FATHER-CHILD

All toddlers struggled to tame their anger at the loved one, all would sometimes forsake their mother and turn to a "better Mommy," and all would tend to fear that in loving two people they might become disloyal to one or the other.

Some fathers had all along participated extensively in the children's early care, either as a regular daily mother substitute or as a second mother (i.e., in a way in which he considered himself as an alternate primary caretaker). In these cases, we learned through their treatment-via-the-parent that this had significantly contributed to the youngsters' heightened difficulty in taming their anger at each loved one. This showed in their marked propensity to control the adults and to experience one parent as "good," the other as "bad," depending on the mood of the moment. Their trouble also showed in their exaggerated loyalty conflict between mother and teachers, as well as at home between the parents, and could often be observed during fathers' visits in the Toddler Group. They might want father to attend to their needs in a way calculated to make mother feel rejected. They might engage father in a game or activity and tell mother to stay away or go to another part of the room. Sometimes they would insist on being bodily close with father and tell him and/or us something bad about mother, such as, "She was mean. She didn't let me wear my new shirt," and at other times they were especially close to mother, and hardly dared to play with father lest their anger at her get the upper hand. These manifestations seemed related to the children's view of the father as a mothering person and were equally evident in cases where the mothering had been prominently shared with a grandmother or housekeeper.

However, even in those cases and at those times when the child viewed the father as a father, and he functioned in this role with mother present, as would often happen at home, and as was the case during his Toddler Group visits, many parents found it difficult to encompass a threesome, with a place for each, and to help their children with it. Not only the children but the parents too behaved in a twosome rather than threesome manner. To an extent this was indirectly referred to before in discussing how we help mothers to understand the role of the teacher and how we approach the work with fathers (chapter 2), as well as in describing some parents' attitude to father substituting for mother in Toddler Group. The fathers' visits highlighted this twosome/threesome issue.

As soon as fathers arrived, many mothers surrendered their own places to them and moved into the background. They did not object to being ignored, did not protest the child's pushing them away, tattling on them to Dad, excluding them from a game, or insisting on father rather than mother taking them to the bathroom. The feeling was sometimes stated that, "This should be their time. I'm so glad they have a chance to be together." It did not occur to the mothers that the child would in the end feel bad for mistreating them and might well fear that the parents' twosome at other times would entail a like disregard for him and his feelings. But even when the child did not try to have Dad to himself, they stepped back, and when the child was reluctant to engage father, they encouraged him to do so and to leave them, instead of helping the child to do something in which all of them could participate. Unconscious anger and resentment no doubt played a part when, as would happen, mothers went so far as to shed their responsibility by not alerting father to our ways and times of doing things, and not helping him or the child with activities with which they, the mothers, were familiar. As a result the fathers and children were suddenly left to their own devices. Fathers found themselves at a loss, did the wrong thing or followed the child's sometimes mistaken lead. The children, in their turn, sometimes took advantage of their fathers' ignorance, felt conflicted, did not really have a nice time with their parents, and missed out on feeling good about themselves.

Complementing the mothers' attitude, the fathers did not try to include the mothers and did not correct or limit their toddlers' disregard for the mothers. Acting on their own, as though they should know all the ropes and be in full command, they did not ask the mothers for help or advice.

Thinking that the parents' behavior was largely caused by the newness of the situation or perhaps a misunderstanding of our expectations, we at first tried not to intercede unless it was really necessary.

> When George suddenly led his father out of the room and mother remained seated looking uneasy, a teacher ran out after them and found them investigating the kitchen, much to the cook's surprise. The father was embarrassed to learn that the children could not usually leave our room during playtime, and that the kitchen could be visited only at specified times. George looked sheepish and later tested several other rules to make sure he would be helped to stay in control.

We soon learned, primarily through the parents' work with their therapist, that at home too there was difficulty in being a threesome, that one or the other parent was expected to be fully in charge. There was little or no support for one another to assure consistency, and the child was not helped to keep the other parent in mind in a loving and thoughtful way. We therefore alerted the mothers to the unhelpful effect of these attitudes during visits, encouraged them to prepare for the visits with father and child, and to remain appropriately involved. We also became more active in assisting them during visits. We involved ourselves in a game or activity with them to show them how they could all play and talk together; we enlisted mother's help and sympathized with father about how hard it was to know one's way about in a new place; we verbalized the child's feelings so that he and the parents could use them to deal better with a given situation.

Tom, 20 months old, as well as his mother and father had been eager for a father visit, and his was among the first scheduled. Mother sat close by, watching but detached as Tom showed Dad his completed favorite puzzle. Father and son then read a book and did a few other things, but father lacked spontaneity and Tom looked increasingly tense and drawn. He then set up the toy animals which he usually paired by mother–baby couples, but this time they were placed randomly. Father tried to participate by talking of where they had seen which animal and what their names were. Tom became more solemn, finally gave up, and just sat disconsolate on the rug between the parents but alone because neither of them knew what was up. I sat down with them and said how sorry I was that Tom looked so sad. I recalled how he usually put the mommy and baby horses and cows together and I wondered if I could help. When I put my hand on the cow and looked around saying, "Where is her child?" Tom perked up with "Can't find her Mommy." He helped me reunite each pair. I commented that sometimes a boy might feel he can't find his Mommy when Daddy comes to visit. Tom nodded "Yes" sadly and, although both parents were still puzzled, got closer to his mother and got a hug.

Discussing this with the parents later, they recognized that their good intention to maximize the opportunity for father–son togetherness had not taken into account that Tom really wanted both parents, that he experienced mother's withdrawal as a rejection, and father's not feeling this with him as a barrier to their relationship. The visit reflected a habitual mode of handling situations but it alerted them to its implications and prompted them to understand and work on this.

During the latter part of the school year we could often see how much the work of parents, therapist, and teachers had paid off. The visits went much better, and parents and children enjoyed themselves more as a family, both in Toddler Group and at home. But for some mothers and fathers progress was slow, in spite of their efforts, because their attitudes were deeply rooted. This exacerbated their children's later difficulties in negotiating the threesome of family relationships, in coping with their own left out feelings, and finding and accepting their place as son or daughter vis-à-vis the parental marital couple. It was therefore especially gratifying to serve some families who could support each other and enjoy their togetherness already during the child's toddlerhood and to be able to help other parents achieve this.

CHAPTER 5

Toileting and the Bodily Self

In the course of healthy development children's emerging life energies make their own contribution to the growing personality. They show in primitive pleasure-seeking and aggressive urges (impulses), and appropriately channeled help with all aspects of zestful living (E. Furman, 1987). At the time, this is not always self-evident, because the child's pleasurable excitement or angry behavior conflict with what the parents consider nice and proper. Depending on the situation and their mood, mothers then characterize their youngster as "ever so positive" or "ever so negative." Their early urges are closely linked to the need-satisfactions of eating and eliminating and to the respective bodily organs, the mouth, anus, and urethra. And urination, so closely associated with the genitals, paves the way for the early sexual impulses of bodily comparison, competition, looking and being looked at. The babies show a predominance of pleasure-seeking and aggressive mouth impulses, the toddlers (with their newly developed sphincter muscles) a predominance of anal and urethral impulses, and the preschoolers focus on early sexual interests. All along, however, there is ample overlap. To start with, all these urges help the child to get to know and like the related body parts, make their use more enjoyable, and protect them from interferences. By bringing

85

about pleasure in living and serving as a guard against hurt, they contribute to survival. With growth and educational help, some of these urges also help in developing desirable traits, such as cleanliness and pity, and others contribute to gender identity and later adult sexuality.

MOUTH IMPULSES

A number of our toddlers showed marked persistence of pleasure-seeking and aggressive mouth impulses as well as conflicts about them, and in each case this related to their special earlier experiences as infants. The manifestations varied. Some used their mouths to explore their environment. Some were greedy with food and materials. They had eating difficulties related to fear of biting people; they did not differentiate between their own and mother's food, or insisted on consuming hers. They bit in anger, especially mother, but sometimes also their blankie or stuffed animal or even their own arm, and chewed on their clothes; they mouthed new toys to investigate them, and tried to ingest inedibles; they stared in an angry eating-up way or could make their open eyes as blank and impenetrable as a tightly closed mouth. Not all of them had all these difficulties. They were intellectually competent and did not lag in most other areas of personality functioning. The intensity and conscious availability of their primitive wishes therefore often surprised and shocked the adults.

> John, 22 months old, brought a cake he and his mother had especially baked to celebrate his birthday early. During playtime before our snack he served his Mom a pretend cake and, persuaded by her, allowed several mother–child couples to join in his party. He kindly gave each a piece of the imaginary cake but refused to take and "eat" a piece himself. Even though encouraged, he desisted. Anticipating the upcoming real birthday snack, the conversation turned on how he had made his real cake. What had he put in? "People," replied John. "No, no, we did not put in paper, dear, the paper was to put under the cake," clarified his mother and then tried again with: "We put in sugar and flour, and what else?" "People," said John, quietly but firmly.

With Mom again explaining about the paper, with the other children anxiously wide-eyed and the mothers in stunned silence, I intervened, saying, "I think John said 'people'." "Yes," nodded John grimly and one of the mothers quickly chimed in "I thought he said 'people', not 'paper'." I asked John whether perhaps it was hard to think of having to share his real and pretend cakes. To this he readily agreed. I then explained that sometimes, when children get very angry they want to put people into the cake instead of giving them cake, and even think about eating them up, but that worries them. Is that so with John, and is that perhaps why he would not eat the pretend cake? John agreed again. He and the others then listened intently as I explained further that these are angry wishes but we don't let them come true. He and Mom made a good safe cake which everyone will enjoy, even John, because he is also proud of his cake and wants to share it in a kind way, in spite of his anger. There was much relief all around and the real party proved a great success.

Although the youngsters with exaggeratedly persisting mouth manifestations received much help and showed much improvement, these early urges and attitudes often burdened their other conflicts during toddlerhood and accompanied them through later development instead of subsiding. For example, some of these youngsters were overeating or not eating during separation from mother at entry to nursery school; their preschool sexual fantasies centered around the use of the mouth; their early conscience was in the image of a devouring monster.

THE MOTHER AND HER TODDLER'S IMPULSES

Regardless of the extent to which the mouth impulses from earlier levels or the sexual impulses from later levels (as will be described) affected the toddlers' thinking and behavior, the mothers sensed, reacted to, and often knew that their children were primarily preoccupied with anal, urinary, and related aggressive wishes and concerns. This preoccupation was not always so evident to other family members, including fathers, or to interested adults outside the family, all of whom tended to be more intrigued with other aspects of growth, such as developing speech or certain skills, or even early sexual manifestations. Not that the mothers disregarded these developments; in fact they sometimes focused on them to deny or to distract themselves and others from their concerns about the child's excretory impulses. Many of the mothers initially acted as though they took their toddlers' messing for granted in a matter-of-fact way, or they attributed its varied manifestations to all kinds of extraneous causes ("a bit tired today"; "a long ride"; "lots of guests last night"; "a cold"; "not used to using a sponge"). Many professed to be quite unconcerned about the child's "getting trained" ("It'll take care of itself"; "he is too young") and, trying to appear relaxed, paid lip service to "the terrible two's." In a setting other than the Toddler Group, they might have used E. G. Smith's (1957) semijocular advice from her *Absolutely Perfect Book of Baby and Child Care*, which is to lie and tell everyone that your child is already clean, because that's what every other mother does anyway.

Yet the most nonchalant mothers with the most laid-back attitude would—sometimes belatedly but always with sincere chagrin—confess to the therapists on episodes of sudden fury and loss of control over a relatively minor incident of the child's soiling or wetting on a rug, leaving his toys around, teasing about getting ready to go out, or about bothering sister or brother. In desperation, the mothers had screamed, punished, or spanked at these times, had withdrawn or banished the child to his room. One usually gentle mother got so upset about her boy spilling some paint that she dumped a ready bucket of water over his head. Another, in a similar situation, walked out, slamming the door, and drove off around the block, not trusting what she would do, and terrifying her suddenly abandoned child. Mothers' true feelings about their toddlers' love of messing run deep and are shared reluctantly, even with those who could empathize and help.

The mothers' upset stemmed, to an extent, from the amount of time and effort necessary to deal with the child's messy and teasing behavior, and from their worry that it would never end and would reflect poorly on their mothering. A less conscious and greater anxiety stemmed from the threat of the toddler's impulses to the habitual ways they, as adults, had learned to repudiate them in themselves. A mother's own early urges and related conflicts are always mobilized in synchrony with her child's phase-appropriate mental experiences to assist her in feeling with him, but the actual day-in-day-out living with him adds to this. She is constantly confronted with him at his level. Many mothers unwittingly become more messy themselves, find themselves spilling things ("I'm getting to be just like him!"), dress less carefully, leave the dishes unwashed, or the toys and clothes lying around. The fathers' most frequently voiced complaint during this period is, "The house is in such a mess when I come home." A few mothers go to the opposite extreme, cleaning constantly, and sometimes even forgetting about the children in the process. The extent to which mothers are enmeshed with their toddlers' elimination is most striking when they watch the child's withholding of urine or bowel movements, suggest perhaps that he should use the toilet or that his body is telling him he needs to use it, and then, time and again, they suddenly have to go to the bathroom themselves. The impact of the child's enjoyment of being mean and cruel can similarly activate their own (see also chapter 7). This threat of or seduction to partial and temporary regression is what makes continuous care of a toddler so difficult. It affects even day care workers, and is one of the reasons why they, like mothers, either have to struggle with their impulses or want to get away from the children. Some of us are fortunate in being less prone to succumb to the onslaught. Many of us benefit by being aware of its pull, and are thereby better able to maintain our adult perspective—something the toddler needs so much from us in order to be able to cope with and master his primitive urges.

There is yet another factor which makes toddler phase impulses so stressful for the mother. When the child's transition from being cared for to self-care was discussed, I stressed the difficult change in the nature of the mother's relationship accompanying the transfer of her ownership of the child's body and its needs to him. The child's impulses are always much more his own, and as they are initially largely linked to need-fulfillment, tend to assert his individuality and to interfere with mother's care of him as a part of herself. During the first year this conflict may show in some mothers' preference for using a pacifier or frequent comfort-nursing, as opposed to letting the child suck his thumb or fingers, and it may also show in their handling of the child's biting at the breast. But these impulse manifestations are usually more readily accommodated through the shared mother–child pleasure in his progression to eating and chewing a variety of foods. During the toddler phase the child's impulses run counter to the mother's expectations and often defy her handling. The toddler's pleasure-seeking and aggressive impulses make her face him as a separate person at a time when she is often not yet ready to acknowledge him as such. Taken aback, mothers often say, "I've lost my baby." When they contrast the child's earlier compliance with his current willfulness or "independence," they often mean primarily his newly active urges. The mother's attitude to her toddler's urges, whether she can let him own them, when and how she gratifies or frustrates them, and the ways in which she helps him to master and use them, will significantly affect not only his ultimate cleanliness but many aspects of his personality growth.

EXCRETORY IMPULSES

Even within the time-limited setting of the Toddler Group there was ample opportunity to observe the manifestations of the toddlers' preoccupation with urinating and passing bowel movements and its impact on their functioning and relationships. With the younger ones the pleasure in "letting go" was prominent. Sometimes, already on arrival, mother would need to change their diapers or pants, saying they had just noticed it and sighing that it was already the third wetting that morning. Shortly thereafter, when I might draw mother's and child's attention to the fact that he seemed to be thinking about something that was going on inside him rather than the toy in front of him, mother would say, "Oh, he couldn't have to pee again!

He just went," but of course he was doing just that and could repeat it several times more through the class session. A sudden withdrawn expression, followed by a beatific smile of pleasure would be a sure sign. With the older toddlers the pleasure in withholding would be more marked. Sometimes on arrival, sometimes later, the children could not start on or continue with their play or activity. They would begin to squirm in their chairs or rock back and forth on their legs on the rug, or want to run around in circles pushing their thighs together, holding their hands to their crotch, bent forward. Their attention span for anything else diminished and their skills disappeared. Suddenly they could not succeed with a familiar task, could not listen to helping instructions, reached for another activity, scattered the toy pieces around them, or rationalized their running around as trying to get another toy.

As the mothers became more aware of what was going on, ceased to encourage their child to persevere with his activity, or to reprimand him for not paying attention, they would instead point out that he needed to use the toilet to feel better. The child would deny and refuse and mother might say, "But you haven't peed since last night," or, "You didn't have a BM yesterday (or since two days ago)!" When they learned that the children would not "feel better" if they eliminated but were enjoying their inner excitement, the mothers were more ready to address this directly, pointing out the need for privacy, and the interference with activities. Sometimes the child would then achieve temporary control and settle down for a bit. Sometimes he eventually relieved himself.

In addition to the spontaneous inner stimulation, almost any available activity (and some more than others, to be sure) could be perceived as an incitement. This was true not only with potentially messy media, such as paints, cleaning with sponges or paper towels, filling flower pots, gluing, washing dishes, watering the plants, pouring juice, or sweeping up crumbs. It applied equally to dumping out the pieces of a puzzle, using glitter to decorate a project, or sugar sprinkles to decorate cookies, even just seeing a pile of blocks, a container with beads, or the shelf with toy plates and cutlery. Often the temptation to stir and scatter or throw such materials around seemed irresistible, and every cleaning up and putting away activity had to be guarded against being turned into an opportunity to mess.

The youngsters who showed a beginning of disgust, with or without some successes in using the toilet, were doubly preoccupied. On the one hand they would notice every speck of dirt or untidiness and then either clean it up or refuse to have anything to do with it. But the next moment they might still indulge in messing. They might avoid painting with a brush but then happily splash water from the dishpan or faucet. The way they used materials often accurately reflected their current attitude to their bodily products and investment of or conflict about their production and disposal. When one little girl started to play in the sandbox, she would pick up a shovel of sand, apparently intent on filling the bucket she had placed in front of herself, but each shovelful inexplicably landed just next to the bucket. Mother's and teacher's help was of no avail, nor were her own repeated efforts. When we shared this observation with the therapist, we learned that the little girl did exactly the same thing in the same persistent way with her bowel movements and urine; she produced them just next to her potty. The use of the water faucet, sprinkling can, and juice pitcher were almost certain indications of a child's attitude to urination. Indiscriminate messing with them, purposeful, gleeful spraying, or pouring in the wrong direction, fear of handling them, careful concentration resulting in partial failure and painful shame, and finally triumphant satisfaction in holding, aiming, and fully succeeding, each reflected parallel periods in the child's attitude to and mastery of his impulses.

The toddlers' messing, of themselves and with activities, was also used to express moods and feelings, especially when the mother could not empathize and understand, or when she withdrew, or when, in her absence, her substitute (father or grandmother) did not feel with and address the child's missing of her. Anger, fear, helplessness, loneliness, envy, overstimulation, and excitement, all could show in heightened preoccupation with anal and urinary matters.

Most striking was the children's use of the mother as they involved her in their excitement and struggles with it. The toddler's angry as well as pleasurable contrariness, teasing, and provocative misbehavior may be seen, from the viewpoint of his personality, as attempts to differentiate himself, to establish and confirm his separateness as an individual. It would be a mistake, however, to disregard the inherent urges which more often than not cause the behavior and are the means whereby the child achieves gratification through it. This is revealed by the frequently visible gleam of excited fun in the child's eyes, the accompanying bodily signs of withholding, the timing of the onset of these episodes with the beginning of his inner preoccupation with anal and urethral sensations, and the parallel crescendo and eventual subsidence of provocative behavior and of holding back and ultimate elimination. The mother is the primary target of the child's "hurting fun" (sadistic enjoyment) and, by being made helpless and angry, is also invited to reciprocate and join the fun. Wetting, soiling, and messing with things is a handy instrument in the tug-of-war, especially when it is known "to get to her"; but any other familiar weakness of hers can also serve this purpose. These interplays are generally well known.

Less widely appreciated is the use of the mother as a partner in sharing or turning inner conflict into fights with her around elimination. One aspect of this is the child "giving" to her the "let go" part of his inner seesaw and keeping the "hold back" part. She then feels the urgency for him and may urge him to "let go," or even has to "let go" for him and suddenly need to use the bathroom herself, as described above. The child then sometimes insists on holding back, and even succeeds in doing so for a while, apparently calmed. At other times, or with another child, there is sudden tremendous upset when mother says, "Well, *I* have to go." As if fearing that the part vested in her would now win out or be returned to him, he screams and cries, clings to her to keep her, or angrily forbids her to enter the bathroom, and if all fails, wants to bang at the closed door. Some children at this stage newly demand to be let in while she is using the bathroom. This may give the appearance of a concern about separation or a wish to view her body and manner of eliminating, but the more immediate reason is the child's need to be with her as a part of his own dealing with his urges.

Her urination and defecation either accomplish it for him or remind him of his inability to use the toilet, and thus act as an affront. As soon as he is helped to know that Mommy's toileting is hers and he will soon want to be boss of his own, his wish to accompany her subsides.

Some youngsters use mother in yet another way. During their holding back/letting go excited inner struggle, the squirming and wiggling is accompanied by messing with things, misbehaving, and irritability. Mother is then apt to put the child on her lap to calm him, and this seems to help until it is noticed that he used the lap time to wet. Mother's containment of the behavioral manifestations resolved the child's inner struggle for him.

TOILET MASTERY

A child's becoming clean and dry may be achieved through "training." The mother wants cleanliness and takes primary responsibility for reading the child's inner signals and rushing him to the potty at appropriate times. Or she may decide to institute a schedule and encourage or force him to sit on the potty at these predetermined times. The mother who "trains" usually also does not expect the child to participate in the dressing and undressing related to toileting or in the cleaning-up process, and she tends to keep for herself the pleasure in success as well as the exasperation of failure, meting out praise or punishment to the child for the extent of his compliance. It is, of course, the mother, rather than the child, who gets trained in this way. Mothers tacitly acknowledge this when, for example, they later blame the child's "accidents" on the nursery school teacher failing to remind the child. Or they assume that just about anything can make him "forget," be it "playing so hard," being tired, not feeling well, not wanting to miss out on story time. The older preschoolers at our Nursery and Kindergarten, as well as the children we consult on in many community centers, usually reveal this kind of earlier training by its unreliability, propensity to regression, and lack of appropriate cleanliness in handling their food, belongings, and use of materials.

At the other extreme, there is anxious fastidious preoccupation with toileting which extends to avoidance or restricted use of many materials. Some of our toddlers' mothers had at some point begun to train in this manner, and then either abandoned the effort before they came to us or, on entry, found themselves in an intense struggle with their child which burdened the relationship.

Toilet mastery is an altogether different approach. Aspects of it were already referred to (chapters 2, 3), such as the utilization and support of the toddler's wish to care for himself, and the many practical ways to facilitate this (standing up for cleaning; encouraging him to clean himself and dispose of the soiled diapers or underpants; dressing him in clothes he can get off and on). Also described were the successive steps in mother–child interaction which lead to doing for oneself and which necessitate a shift in the mother's investment so that she can let the child own his body and its needs as well as the satisfaction in his achievements. The importance was mentioned of helping the child with the use of materials and activities to channel his impulses and find pleasure in nonbodily pursuits and, above all, of the gradual establishment of the "turnaround" which turns the wish to be dirty into the wish to be clean.

Acquiring the wish to be clean is a pivotal step. On the one hand it prompts the child's efforts at being clean and enables him to use them and the success they bring to build his self-esteem; on the other hand, it helps him to master impulses by transforming and using their energy to enrich areas of functioning and to pave the path toward independence. The turnaround of disgust at dirt—part of the wish to be clean—is potentially most helpful and adaptive when it comes about in identification with the mother and is part of the loving admiring wish to be like her. In contrast to a mother's marked lack of abstemiousness in regard to her nursling's bowel movements prior to the introduction of mixed foods, she usually and quite involuntarily registers at least facial disgust at cleaning up her older infant or toddler. She keeps herself at arm's length from him, and often then hugs him with a happy smile when the job is finished, "Oh, you smell so nice and clean now." Gazing at her through all this, infants often imitate mother's grimace of disgust and later on may look disgusted even as they indulge in smelling at the dirty diapers or swishing around their soiled clothes in the bucket or toilet bowl.

> One 14-month-old not only made a disgusted face at bowel movements but carefully noted and picked up any trash she could find and disposed of it in the wastebasket. Yet at the dinner table, when she joined the family in eating hot dogs, this same precociously verbal little girl pointed to the mustard pot, saying "Pass the BM, please." Her three years older sister saved the day by passing the mustard and explaining calmly, "It's mustard, we don't eat BMs."

Most of our toddlers showed signs of beginning disgust before they applied it fully to mastering toileting. They showed disgust at other people's messes. They were hesitant to use messy media, or needed a sponge right near to wipe off dirt which accidentally got on their hands. They showed delight in making things tidy and clean. They took care not to spill or mess with their food. Mothers and teachers would use these opportunities to acknowledge how nice it is to be clean and link this to toileting: "Soon you will want to put your pee and BM in the toilet so you can keep all clean." This link needs to be made because a growing "turnaround" can remain isolated from toileting, either to allow the child to continue to indulge in messing in this area, and/or because his disgust is so extreme that he refuses to have anything to do with his messes and their clean-up.

> At over 2 years of age, Holly still wet and soiled at home and insisted on mother doing all the cleaning. She refused to touch potentially messy things in Toddler Group and became hysterically upset over a little bit of wet sand which got on her shoe in the playground. Unable to bear this dirt on her clothing, Holly screamed and sobbed in her mother's arms while the teacher washed off the shoe. She did not calm down until she saw her shoe was all clean again. We learned that the mother's own exaggerated concern over dirt had contributed to Holly's, but the child's upset was also caused by displaced feelings about her ongoing messing with elimination.

Mother helped by acknowledging and apologizing for her own excessive disgust as well as by hoping Holly would not have to be quite like herself in this respect. She further helped Holly to distinguish between excrements and other dirt, and initiated with her activities such as making things of playdough and sand. At the same time, she began to address Holly's ongoing soiling and wetting, pointing out that this really made her dirty and couldn't fail to bother her, and she suggested that Holly's big upset over other dirt belonged perhaps to feeling bad about the toileting messes. Mother engaged Holly in cleaning up herself and her clothes. When Holly complained that she didn't want to touch that dirt and get it on her hands, mother agreed that she herself did not like it and therefore did not mess on herself. Holly could avoid touching it too if she used the toilet, but until she was ready to do so, the mess was Holly's, not Mom's.

Although Holly now began to enjoy her activities more, she also became more angry and defiant with mother, and one day, after a period of evident withholding, made a big puddle on the floor. She was beside herself with shame and fury, could hardly be induced to help with the clean-up, yelled at anyone who came near, and then hid away, in spite of reassurance that she was still a nice girl and would soon succeed in keeping herself clean. This incident was a turning point in Holly owning her inner struggle, and she did indeed soon succeed in mastering it.

The child's own feelings and means of coping are not a replica of the mother's, but the nature of her attitude to dirt plays an important part. Whereas Holly's mother's attitude to dirt was excessive, some mothers' attitude to dirt was inconsistent, combining, for example, angry anxiety over elimination with encouraging the child to wallow in sand or to mess with paints, usually without noticing his discomfort at the mixed messages. Some mothers lacked a sufficient all-round sense for cleanliness and tidiness, and others objected to dirt as though it were an aggressive assault. For example, when a splotch of washable paint accidentally landed on one mother's skirt, she reacted with, "Now look what you've done! You've ruined it for good!" She was, incidentally, a mother who was not tidy herself and professed lack of concern over her child's toileting.

At best, turning love of messing into the opposite love of cleanliness and disgust at dirt, and putting this to use in mastering toileting is a long process, with ups and downs over a period of several months. It is a hard inner struggle for the child, one in which his wanting to succeed is often far ahead of his ability to do so. As a result, there are many moments of deep frustration with himself, loss of self-esteem, shame vis-à-vis others, and hopelessness about ever making it. This, in turn, leads many times to a temptation to turn the inner conflict into an outer fight and to give mother the part that wants to be clean, is responsible for making the effort, and should bear the pain and anger at failure. It is very important, therefore, for the mother to stand by all along and assist her child in recognizing all parts of his struggle as his own and in empathizing with, but not taking over, his feelings about his successes and failures. At all times too, she has to trust implicitly and explicitly in his ultimate mastery. The mother's attitude to mastery is crucial, in this as in all her child's undertakings. If she doubts him, falls into despair, does not believe that repeated effort can lead to success, even though she has actually succeeded in getting clean and knows that everyone else has, how can she lend some perspective to his predicament?

Mastery of toileting requires a lot of the child, apart from the skills of dressing and cleaning and acquiring a love of cleanliness, although these are among the signs of his readiness to address the task. It also involves perception and understanding of inner bodily sensations and the sense of time that makes it possible to anticipate an event and to act in light of that recognition. Initially, when the children register their internal signals of pending elimination, they often attribute them to a different need. Some children think they are hungry or thirsty.

> Nina always asked for a drink of water, much to her mother's puzzlement about her child's excessive thirst. Even the mother was not aware that these requests always coincided with the beginning of squirming until we pointed this out. The mother then quickly confirmed this for herself and alerted Nina, "I think it feels like you need a drink but your body is really telling you that it's time to do pee-pee." For a moment the little girl's face had a bewildered look, then she had an inward look, and said, "Oh" in recognition.

Other youngsters suddenly "need" this, that, and the other toy or material, jerking their arms here and there to point to all they want. Of course, no item satisfies them, and the demandingness crescendoes along with the wiggling, and usually ends up with wet pants. With some children the bodily signals are clearly visible to everyone, but mother pointing them out meets with unawareness or denial until the child is helped to acknowledge and evaluate them as his own.

However, knowing and owning his inner prompters does not necessarily lead to eliminating. Even the child who really wants to keep clean misjudges how long he can hold back. He will indulge in "playing" with the internal sensations, and then either has to make a sudden last-minute dash to the bathroom or wets his pants a bit just as he starts to use the toilet. Alternatively, he misses the right time altogether and simply wets or soils himself. The child's ability to anticipate and time his elimination is so limited that, for a long time, mothers keep a potty ready on each floor, carry it in the car, and know every bathroom in every store they go to. Mothers also help the sense of time a lot by talking about the future: "*Soon* you will tell me before it comes. Soon you'll let yourself know in time and then you'll really manage to keep clean." It is just about impossible for toddlers to anticipate the far future, such as a long car ride or shopping expedition, and to use the toilet ahead of time when they feel as yet no urgency at all.

TOILETING AND EARLY SEXUAL CONCERNS

With all toddlers the wish to be like the parent is a prominent part of their efforts at toileting. This always involves a measure of wanting to be "big." There is a considerable difference, however, in whether the mother and child view being big in terms of being clean or mainly in terms of power and performance to impress. In the latter case there is little teaching and acquiring of a "turnaround" from love of dirt to disgust at it. The emphasis, instead, is on showing the child how the grown-ups and older siblings urinate, defecate, and bathe or shower.

Our data indicate that these children, although they also become clean and dry, tend to miss out on the enriching aspects of a love of cleanliness and dislike of dirt, such as the proud extension of keeping clean to their belongings, room, and tidy but creative use of materials. They also tend to miss out on the sense of mastery which stems not just from control of elimination but from the personality's gain through having diverted and transformed impulse energy for its own use. Their anal and urinary excitements are equally intense and more prolonged, and the achievement of mastery is burdened by heightened concerns over adequacy, competitive comparison, and sexual differences.

When the child who primarily wants to be "big" messes himself, he regards himself as little and stupid rather than as dirty or smelly. There is little impetus to take care of cleaning himself up because making himself clean and good-smelling does not amend the failure, cannot help to restore a good feeling about himself. He has to wait to prove himself "big" until the next time he eliminates. In the meantime he feels inadequate. In his disgruntlement with himself, he may want to prove himself big in magic ways which contribute nothing to his self-esteem in a lasting way (such as belittling others, demanding big things, showing off defensively, eating big amounts of food), or he may try to avoid feeling incompetent by restricting his involvement with skills and activities, or even resort to pathological symptomatic solutions.

Different forms of interplay between early sexual concerns and toileting are illustrated by the case of Sally (chapter 3) who viewed the diapers as bodily appendages, a substitute for the desired penis, and by T. Barrett's report on Candy (chapter 6). Tessa showed some individual responses and some which were shared by a number of other children.

Tessa, 2 years old, had known her inner elimination signals for several months and reported them to her mother, but had not shown any effort at toilet mastery and did not in the least protest mother's diapering of her. At home this was done in a prone position, often in front of her brother and visitors. In Toddler Group, whenever she was about to wet herself, she would lie on her back with her feet up in the air and expose her lower parts. Her play with dolls looked caring and maternal except for moments of harsh yanking at their clothes. In this connection Tessa told of the baby boy whom she watched being diapered at her sitter's home, but Tessa had also seen her sibling and parents in the nude and during toileting. She had been talked to, rather than with, about sexual differences, and been given the words for male and female genitals which she apparently accepted.

One day we watched Tessa furiously grabbing and pushing at the crotch of a boy doll. This was a dressing doll, some of whose garments could be removed and put on to practice zippers, buttons, and snaps, but its pants, which characterized it as a boy, did not come off and it had no explicit sexual markings. When asked about her persistent attacks on the doll's clothed crotch, Tessa said, "I am just changing him." On further questioning, she added rather guiltily "into a girl." During the same period, she was also preoccupied with a loosely capped hole in our sink top where a drinking fountain had been removed. In spite of repeated explanations, she kept on asking about it, taking off the cap, and trying to fill it with other longer objects which never quite fit. She repeated this with increasing anger and insistence.

We pointed out her worry about the hole as well as her angry "changing" of the doll, and alerted mother, who then took it up in the treatment-via-the-parent. Mother–child discussion about the double meaning of "changing" shed light on Tessa's compliance with being diapered and reluctance to use her own "hole" to toilet independently. Her anger at the boys and fear of male visitors (she was glad to have her father) could now also be addressed, as well as her avoidance of the many activities which she feared would reveal her bodily inadequacy. Tessa began to voice her feelings about sexual differences and, with mother better able to hear and respond, her toileting, zest for activities, and self-esteem improved.

Apparent lack of interest in toilet mastery and acquiescence in mother's ministrations were frequent signs of underlying concerns about adequacy in boys as well as girls.

"AM I ALL RIGHT?"

In addition to the effect on their toileting, the toddlers who had observed the sexual differences showed their feelings and concerns about this in many other areas of functioning. Some felt so inadequate that they simply did not want to be themselves. One little girl introduced herself to a visitor by the name of her older, more accomplished sister. Another persistently wanted to be either a baby or an adult, showing this, for example, at home meals by insisting on using either her outgrown highchair or a chair for grown-ups, but refusing to sit in the youth chair which was most appropriate for her size. One boy acted this out by alternately adopting whiney baby talk and strutting around in macho fashion, and another showed it by wanting to wear a mask. Several youngsters became very upset and angry when they could not wear clothing items they associated with the more desirable other sex or adult body. Some had to equip themselves with accessories which would, in their eyes, change their status.

As already mentioned, most of these youngsters extended their feelings of inadequacy to their attitude to activities. Some avoided them or restricted themselves to what they felt they could do well, or they destroyed their productions because they considered them not good enough. Particularly striking, however, was their worry that their performance would not show up well by comparison with others or would be judged inferior. They were preoccupied with looking at everything the others did. Some even peeked intrusively. Yet they became very upset about being looked at. Some hid whatever they were working on and angrily refused to show it to teachers or peers even when they were doing very well with it by objective standards. Some, like Tim (chapter 3), discontinued their activity when others were practicing it at the same time. One boy boasted at home about all the wonderful things he made in Toddler Group but refused to take them home to show, or crumpled them up before reaching home. Another told us of all the wonderful things he made at home but refused to bring them to show at school.

Even when they could be helped to know and verbalize feeling little, stupid, and ashamed as well as envious and angry at those they considered more perfect, they still could not imagine that their own efforts could lead to improvement, much less to the desired goal. They would either have to pretend to be superadequate or grab others' "know-how" for themselves, or destroy what the others had. Sometimes these impulses were acted out. More often they showed indirectly, by a refusal or stubborn misuse of help or by irritably demanding that their mothers should do it for them. Their inner fury and lack of trust in their own means of mastery made constructive learning impossible.

The link between these difficulties and the bodily concerns was usually revealed through the work of treatment-via-the-parent. For example, the parents would begin to notice the similarity between the child's conflict over looking and being looked at in school, and his insistence on looking at the parents in the nude during dressing and toileting, but insisting on privacy for himself. Often though, the link could also be observed in Toddler Group. In the midst of hiding their work on a puzzle or other activity, they would suddenly have to show us a quite minor or even imaginary hurt or defect on their hand or other body part, perhaps an old little scratch, a nonexistent spot, or a bit of peeling skin. Or they would, out of the blue, talk about having a (usually mispronounced) vagina or would touch their penis in an anxious way.

As the parents became more aware of the children's concerns and could empathize better with their feelings, they also observed more closely the behavioral responses to the sight of others' nudity and decided that these encounters were beyond the children's capacity for integration. On the basis of this understanding, rather than by complying with the professionals' advice, they could then discuss it with their youngsters, prepare them for instituting all-round privacy in the home, and protect them from exposure elsewhere. Mostly, the toddlers responded with relief. The new regime opened the path for verbal parent–child communication and clarification and led to better mastery (including toileting), improved self-esteem, and a markedly changed attitude to learning and involvement in activities. I wish to stress that it was not the mere closing of doors but the fact that it was one of the results of the parents' better ability to feel with their children which made the difference.

Sadly, some parents could not be helped to feel with their children in this respect, or did so only in such a half-hearted way that they did not consistently protect them from exposure to nudity and/or failed to note the child's response when it happened. When one little girl returned with renewed symptoms after a brief holiday, we wondered with her mother what the child had experienced. The mother acknowledged that a male relative had exposed himself, but was amazed that we had seen the connection. She had denied it to herself, although she, the therapist, and we had traced these links many times. These children's related difficulties did not improve much and their troubled feelings significantly burdened their later development.

Some of our toddlers had not observed others' bodies and it was helpful to compare their very different attitudes. Chris was one of them.

According to his mother, Chris had clearly been a boy in his own and others' view as early as 10 months old. Other than from general appearance and manner of movement, she judged this by his closeness to his Dad and delight in having things like Dad; for example, carrying around a briefcase, filling it with papers, and often taking them out to scribble on them, and then putting them back and closing up the briefcase, all in obvious imitation of his father. Later, as a young toddler, Chris delighted in cooking and cleaning with his Mom and he cared for his teddy and other stuffed animals in a maternal way, all just like Mom. But he very much missed his father when the latter was at work and nothing thrilled him more than to be with Dad doing "Daddy things" on weekends. He initiated efforts at self-care early, and when he began to work on toilet mastery he became pleasurably fascinated with faucets and spent much time pouring water into and out of containers during his bath and at the sink. Watering cans and anything that had spouts were the favorites. At the same time, machinery of every kind, but especially large machines, worked by men, became a special interest. He soon differentiated the garbage trucks, power shovels, backhoes, cement trucks, and tractors, and was especially happy when he was allowed to sit for a while in the driver's seat of one of these parked vehicles. He achieved toilet mastery at 23 months. By this time he could independently direct his urine stream, and asked about his testicles and scrotum, and integrated the whole organ into his body-image.

Shortly after, and having observed the neighborhood children draw their body outlines in chalk on the pavement, he asked for help in similarly drawing the outlines of his mother, father, and himself. They did. Chris then took the chalk and drew on his outline a longish loop between the thighs and, when asked about this, said it was his penis. He was concerned when he learned that the rain would wash away all the drawings, but readily accepted the assurance that this would affect only the drawing and that his body would remain safe.

Throughout, Chris had shown the same initiative and wish to master activities other than those related to self-care. There was one difference. With toileting Chris was completely private, although he readily showed his achievements in play and activities to others and was pleased when they shared his pride in them. Of course, this too was no doubt an identification with his parents. They kept their dressing and toileting private. Chris had never seen them or anyone else, adult or child, in the nude or eliminating. He clearly differentiated men from women and boys from girls, had clearly invested his own excretory organs in a loving way, and had not shown concern over the secondary sexual characteristics he had observed, although he had, all through his second year, been very aware of all differences. Questions and concern arose in those instances where he thought something or somebody was hurt or damaged, for example, people with a cane or in a wheelchair, a bandage or obvious sore on someone's body, a dead insect. Answers helped him and he did not fear for his own integrity. When he himself was hurt, ill, or unable to do something, he asked for help or persisted in his efforts, or got angrily frustrated, but it did not shatter his overall self-regard and self-esteem.

No doubt, Chris's confident and pleasurable investment of himself and his ability to master were not solely due to not having to cope with the impact of sexual differences, but were related to his parents' being in tune with him and adjusting their handling accordingly. The importance of the parents being in tune was stressed also by T.-B. Hägglund (1987). In his country, Finland, the custom of the family sauna exposes all prepubertal children to the parents' and siblings' bodily differences and, in doing so, has an inevitable effect on them. The

milieu of the sauna is traditionally calm, without excited interplays or mutual touching. According to Hägglund, the children's ability to cope with the stimulating experience, with their
concerns, questions, and feelings, and to integrate them to a
sufficient extent, depends primarily on the parents' awareness
of their youngsters' responses, capacity to empathize, and to
address the issues in a reassuring and clarifying manner.

Unfortunately, our toddlers' experiences of viewing others'
bodies took place in a very different milieu. As described earlier
(chapter 4), many of our toddlers showed early sexual excitement and behavior with their fathers during visits, and with
some this was also true of their behavior with their mothers. In
these instances, the parents initiated and enjoyed this form of
interaction. At home it was present to a much greater extent.
On the fathers' part it included tickling and roughhousing,
chasing games, and excited hugging and bouncing. Mothers
would show it by excessive fondling, kissing the child's body,
and by overly stimulating cleansing ministrations, with the child
in a passive position. There were excited games among siblings
of both sexes which sometimes included excited exhibiting and
touching. Toddlers often shared the siblings' and/or parents'
beds, and several children had observed sexual intercourse. In
such a milieu, viewing the parents' and siblings' dressing and
toileting implied a measure of excitement on everyone's part,
even when the adults were unaware of their own feelings, and
either disregarded or punished the children's responses. Except for their tendency to excited interactions and signs of sexual overstimulation, some of our toddlers seemed to take all
this in stride until they were confronted with the sexual differences away from home, as with relatives, at a sitter's, or in a
group setting. As if such additional exposures were the straw
that broke the camel's back, they often caused major concerns
and were the first to bring a flood of anxious questions and
responses.

We also had a few toddlers whose overstimulation resulted
from illness and medical–surgical procedures, such as bodily
anomalies or repeated bladder infections, and related interventions, such as tests, surgery, catheterization.

And there were a few youngsters whose manifest early sexual excitement was primarily a well-tested means of engaging and holding the parent's interest and attention. It would give way quite abruptly to sad and pained loneliness when the parent lost interest and turned away, or it switched to trying to recapture him or her in another way, perhaps through teasing or misbehavior. Mostly, this excitement subsided altogether when the parent could be helped to relate with the child in a more consistent and more neutrally affectionate manner.

Regardless of the cause of the overstimulation, the children's intense excitement did not give them pleasurable satisfaction and did not help them to enjoy, integrate, and feel good about their genitals. On the contrary, masturbation caused them conflict, sometimes fear of hurting themselves or of having damaged themselves, and in some cases, became compulsive and hence symptomatic. Instead of helping them to integrate their sexual organs, the excitement appeared to increase their unhappiness about them. Most of the children could be helped through treatment-via-the-parent, but only because work on these topics continued through their preschool years when the earlier experiences and concerns were seen to have contributed to difficulty in coping with the later developmental tasks. This contrasted markedly with children like Chris who invested and enjoyed his penis as a urinary rather than genital organ, and whose pleasurable excitement was of a urinary rather than genital nature.

THE URGES AND THE INVESTMENT OF THE BODILY SELF

Some parents thought that by introducing their young toddler to sexual differences calmly and casually, the child would accept them in a matter-of-fact way and the potential for secrecy and excitement would be avoided.

Annie, 14 months old, visited with her mother a family friend who had a 3-month-old son. While the baby's mother changed

his diapers, Annie saw his penis and asked about it. It was Annie's first such observation and her mother told her it was a penis
and that's what made the baby a boy. That night Annie called
out in her sleep "Johnny not boy," woke terrified and upset, and
had to be comforted by her Mom. This prompted the mother
to seek professional advice. Our subsequent work revealed that
Annie, who was in the midst of getting to know her own urinary
function by enjoying letting go, had experienced the boy's different body as a deep hurt to her self-regard.

Different toddlers respond differently to such first experiences, depending on the parent's presence or absence and way
of handling it, and depending also on the exact details of the
experience. Regardless of the nature of the response, however,
and even when the experience is mitigated and helped by the
presence and emotional availability of the mother, the perception of the manifest difference affects the child's loving investment of his or her own body and comparable body parts.

In describing our educational policies (chapter 2), I
stressed our experience that all toddlers are acutely observant
of the most minute bodily differences and variations, and noted
how we help them cope with their concerns. This is not a sign
of their curious and excited sexual interest but reflects, I believe, the fragility of the young child's concept of his body and
of his loving investment in it, all at a time when he is in the
process of making his body his own and begins to want to
exercise control over its functions and care. The toddler's vulnerability is further heightened by his new awareness of all that
he cannot do, of his helplessness, and of his need of mother's
help and willingness to help.

The early urges and the pleasure they bring are of enormous help with this. During infancy the mouth impulses assist
the child in investing his mouth and eating, which are crucial
to survival. During the toddler phase, the anal and urinary
impulses serve to invest and enjoy these body parts and their
important excretory functions. The toddler experiences these
organs and their sensations as excretory, not as sexual. The
penis is for urinating, as is the girl's urethra, and insofar as
they evoke genital sensations, these are secondary. The accompanying interests and play (building towers, forming enclosures

with blocks, making playdough "sausages," pouring from pitchers and sprinkling cans, playing with faucets) as well as the pride and pleasure in control and mastery, may *look* like early sexual manifestations. However, when they are understood in the wider context of the child's verbalizations, behavior, and relationships, they clearly signify primarily anal and urinary impulses and ways of dealing with them, and are related to the respective inner sensations and excretory functions of the bodily organs. As a result, the exposure to others' excretory organs and their different ways of eliminating, above all threatens the toddler's phase-appropriate attempt to own and invest his excretory organs and functions in a loving way, and constitutes a greater or lesser injury to his self-regard. Just as we are often especially upset about the least spot on a new dress or scratch on a new car, so the toddler is appalled to find that his newly owned body and its functions appear flawed or endangered when he is faced with comparisons. Moreover, in his global way of thinking and feeling, one thing wrong means everything is wrong. It is not just a part of him that is not perfect, all of him feels inferior. Once he has coped with the developmental task and established pleasurable confidence in ownership and mastery of function, seeing others look and do differently is much less disturbing and much easier to understand and integrate.

When the toddler, especially the young toddler, is not only exposed to others' different bodies and ways of eliminating but is subjected to experiences which specifically stimulate early sexual sensations before he has dealt with his excretory impulses, he is much less able to cope. His self-love is diminished, his anger is heightened. It's like having to learn third grade lessons when one is still in first grade.

CHAPTER 6

Candy Masters Toileting

Thomas F. Barrett, Ph.D.

Prior to their application to the Hanna Perkins Toddler Program on Candy's behalf, Candy's parents had dealt with many sad experiences with their older children. It was in conjunction with these experiences and their aftermath that the parents had first sought consultation with the therapist.

Candy had been a wanted and beloved baby, but her first year had been somewhat overshadowed by her parents' concerns. Her development had been slow. She did not walk until 17 months, had few words, and did not yet use them for communication at her time of entry into the Toddler Program. As a result, she did not often make her presence felt within the family. The parents had become aware of this and wanted to help her develop and enjoy herself. For this reason they applied to Hanna Perkins.

When Candy began at Toddler Group at 1 year, 11 months, she would arrive well groomed, but soon become messy, especially at snack time. She would take a mouthful of juice and then let it dribble down her chin and onto her clothes, and she deliberately poured juice on her cookie. There was no evidence of a reaction formation to dirt. During the weeks that followed, Candy's mother reported that she had thought about toilet training but, expecting trouble, had not taken any steps. She and the therapist talked of how it was helpful for a toddler to be supported in developing a dislike for messiness. Mother acknowledged that her own dislike of messes usually resulted in her avoiding, quickly cleaning, or removing any untidiness. Consequently, Candy had not had much exposure to clean-up opportunities. Mother avoided giving Candy any messy foods and had not let Candy try media like paint or playdough. She also took full charge of diaper changes. Through this discussion with the therapist, and encouraged by her observations and experiences at Toddler Group with handling and talking about messing and cleaning, mother became more able to allow Candy's participation and shared in her child's resulting pleasures at active mastery.

Soon, there were signs of a developing dislike of dirt. Though Candy's messiness at table persisted for a time, and although when painting she initially got paint on her hair, face, and clothes without evident discomfort, she began to wipe glue from her fingers and seemed not to like the sticky feel. On the day when her second birthday was celebrated, she managed well at snack, could pass the cookies she'd brought, and enjoyed giving and receiving gifts.

From the outset of the work it was clear that mother had entered the developmental phase of parenthood. At times though, she seemed a bit out of sync with Candy. Occasionally she would do things for Candy which the child could actually do for herself. For example, she might quickly wipe Candy's mouth at snack time or might hold her on a swing or teeter seat as if she were a much younger child who could not sit securely on her own. At other times mother could seem distracted or preoccupied. Candy angrily protested mother's infantile care and often responded to her periods of withdrawal by getting into trouble as a way of regaining her investment. Mother became aware of her difficulty, and found it helpful when she could talk with the therapist about some worries remaining from painful experiences endured with some of her older children. Following on this work she seemed more confident in supporting Candy's striving toward mastery, and she was realistically thoughtful about Candy's safety needs.

The work particularly focused on ways mother could help support Candy's efforts at mastery in self-care skills. Candy got on well with them, including toilet mastery. At first, teaching disgust and assisting Candy to clean up for herself, seemed hard work for mother. However, she was now more observant of Candy's wish to be clean, and her ability to help in clean-up efforts, and she was also more aware of her own reluctance to help Candy grow up. Again, she was able to acknowledge that past experiences had left her with worries and, as a result, she tended not to think of her daughter as a unique person in her own right, someone with her own likes, dislikes, opinions, or ideas, especially if these might contrast with mother's own. Candy's mother could show pride and pleasure in some of her daughter's achievements (e.g., dressing, speech) but she showed exasperated anger in responses to Candy's wishes for independence, viewed by mother at times as anger against her. Mother acknowledged it was hard for her to watch Candy grow up as she expected Candy to be her last child. This was discussed with the therapist and as these feelings were verbalized, mother became more able to be helpful to Candy. She took care to prepare Candy for changes or transitions, she listened to Candy, she could better feel with her and help Candy find words for her feelings, and Candy increasingly used words instead of action.

With greater autonomy, Candy also began to experience more conflict about her toileting. She dealt with this by withholding and involving mother. At first she wiggled and was restless at snack. Mother thought Candy was tired and offered her a brief rest on her lap. Candy snuggled in, wet herself, and felt relieved. When mother discontinued the lap sitting and pointed out Candy's withholding, Candy gave mother the task of worrying about wetting. This was especially evident one day at Toddler Group as she seemed contrary and unable to let herself fully enjoy or participate in activities. The more mother encouraged Candy to try the potty, the more Candy remained resistant. Finally, mother decided she herself needed to use the restroom, so it was arranged that a teacher would wait outside the door with Candy. No sooner was mother out of sight than Candy burst into angry tears. It seemed evident that she had been depending upon mother's participation in the struggle. Candy calmed down when her teacher assured her that soon she would feel she could be the boss of her own "pee-pee" and take care of it, just as mommy took care of her own.

Mother found helpful the work with the therapist and the supportive comments of the teachers. She could recognize Candy's increased aversion to being messy and her readiness to progress with toilet mastery. Nevertheless, her enduring wish to keep Candy little and dependent continued to interfere with her being able to let Candy take a more active role and participate in the changing process. Following on talks with the therapist, mother tried to pursue a plan to have Candy out of diapers and into panties. However, at first it remained hard for her to differentiate between what were internal and external struggles for Candy. One day at Toddler Group Candy made butterscotch pudding. She was a happy and proud participant, cleaned up well, and enjoyed the pudding for snack. Near the end of snack though she became silly and had trouble staying in her chair. The squirming seemed a clue that Candy needed to use the bathroom. Mother was helped to note this connection when a teacher commented that Candy might soon want to let herself use the toilet so that all the wiggling would not get in the way of her fun with doing things.

Through the work with the therapist mother was specifically encouraged to abandon the use of a changing table so Candy could stand and help with diapering, cleaning of herself, and disposal of her messy diapers. Mother protested that Candy would just run off as she often did when mother took her to the grocery store. Gradually though, Candy's mother could try these changes and there were initial successes. Candy liked being clean and dry and was happy with her "pretty panties." She was dry for several days, but Mother still found it hard at times to let Candy be the one to have the feeling about either her proud successes or unhappy failures.

She also tended to hover or try to do too much to help, conveying the unspoken message to Candy that she would not succeed. One day before Toddler Group the therapist observed mother and Candy in the hallway outside the classroom. With mother in close pursuit, Candy, with a large backpack on her back, dashed down the hall and made a sharp turn into a storage closet, mistaking it for the restroom. When mother saw the therapist she said, "We have our big girl pants today." Candy then dashed back up the hall, dropping her backpack as she went and when she got to the water fountain she climbed on the stool in front of it and made the water come out as if to illustrate her own wish (but also conflict) about voiding. Later, in Toddler Group, it was revealed that the backpack was filled with several extra pairs of panties.

For a time, as Candy became more interested in using the toilet it seemed mother was not always ready to be supportive. She complained Candy developed chronic diarrhea and so put Candy back in diapers. Following this, Candy again had some dry days. She was dry all day at an extended family gathering, but woke up ill with vomiting the next morning. Mother was worried by the emesis and the mess it made, and in her anxiety she held Candy over the toilet with her face close to the bowl, encouraging her to vomit into it, which Candy was unable to do. For several days thereafter Candy seemed afraid of the toilet, and could only resume using it after mother talked with the therapist about what had occurred, understood this as the origin of the worry, and then talked with Candy about how scary and confusing it was to have been sick, and have mother hold her over the toilet.

Candy's efforts at toilet mastery were also complicated by bodily concerns which were first revealed in excited closeness she initiated with father when he visited at Toddler Group. Later, it was observed that Candy flirted with other fathers who visited, and she responded to a male peer's father visiting by being unusually aggressive toward the boy and enviously wanting to have for her own use any of the toys the boy tried to use in his play with his father. It was learned that, at times, mother had not been private with Candy regarding bathroom activities. She had allowed Candy into the bathroom with her and had not shielded Candy from exposure to nudity displayed by other family members. When the therapist worked with mother around the benefits of helping to establish more privacy for everyone at home, including the older children, mother was at first perplexed when Candy was angry at being suddenly shut out of mother's toileting. Gradually it became apparent that Candy's anger had been a response to feeling she was being kept out in a way that made her feel she was being rejected by her mom. Mother reassured Candy this was not the case. She began to talk with Candy about how it could feel good to be private and modest. Mother and father also worked on this for themselves and encouraged the older children to be private as well. Over time, mother was able to help Candy find pleasure in having her own space, including her own privacy, and she supported Candy's verbalized requests for this at home.

Candy was now less aggressively excited and her investment in neutral activities increased. She also ceased to restrict her visual perception, a defense which we had not previously recognized (e.g., she used not to look at certain visitors but now did look at them with manifest fear). One visitor seemed to remind her of the nurse at her doctor's office and was associated with blood tests. In other situations too Candy began to bring her bodily integrity worries in a displaced way. She showed concern about what was thrown away in the wastebasket at Toddler Group and needed her teacher's promise that she would watch over Candy's belongings and keep them safe while Candy went to the bathroom. Also, she wanted to take a large pinecone into the bathroom with her and became "show-offy" regarding her clothes and belongings. Mother told the therapist that at home Candy showed a fearful response when her grandfather injured his foot and needed to keep it bandaged. Mother and father, who also often attended conferences with the therapist, found it helpful to understand how Candy's efforts at achieving toilet mastery were complicated by concerns arising from her observations of sexual differences, and by excessive stimulation, engendered by excited roughhousing with her brother. Increasingly, they could talk with Candy about how her body was just right as it was. They reassured her of her safety and supported her verbalizations of protest whenever her brother wanted to play too aggressively. Though there were still lapses of privacy at home, particularly involving the older children entering the parents' bedroom or bath, Candy's demand of "me have privacy" was supported by the parents, and the older siblings were kept out when she was in the bathroom.

By the end of Toddler Group it was observed that self-care efforts had proceeded with Candy showing good, self-motivated dressing skills, good table manners (including cleanliness at table and careful pouring, about which she was proud). Washing and clean-up efforts showed increased reaction formation to dirt, and by the summer following Toddler Group, toilet mastery appeared complete and autonomous.

CHAPTER 7

Coping with Aggression

THE FEAR OF AGGRESSION

The toddler's aggression is, to him and to his mother, as much a vital part of daily life as are the pleasure-seeking anal and urinary impulses. Coping with his aggression in ways that serve his personality growth is a most important developmental task during this phase. It affects all aspects of functioning as well as the child's chances of dealing with the conflicts that lie ahead. The toddler's own concern with aggression is different and more immediate. It shows strikingly in the child's ever present alert attention to the feelings and manifestations of anger in others and to situations in which others might be "mean." Nothing brings the entire group's activity to a halt as much as one child's angry outburst, and nothing rivets their attention on that child's mother and on the teacher as much as the expectation of the adults' response. The occasional distant yells of an angry nursery schooler, heard from the hall, always prompt anxious questions. If a fly or a little bug appears in the room, everyone watches to see whether or how it might be disposed of. The least damage to materials and equipment is pointed out as the possible result of somebody's destructiveness. But the very rare moments when a mother might speak harshly to her child are seemingly ignored, and would remain unquestioned if we did not address them. Obviously, a mother's anger is by far the

119

worst example of aggression, too threatening for toddlers to contemplate.

Many factors motivate the children's fascinated concern, in different measure at different times. There is the still age-appropriate difficulty in differentiating between self and other, so that anyone's anger could be one's own. There is the worry of aggression getting out of control and hurting or overwhelming self and others. There is the sadistic ("hurting fun") enjoyment, or expectation of enjoyment, and sometimes vicarious enjoyment. There are the beginnings of righteous condemnation and the threat to recently developed means of taming aggression. Regardless of which factor may be uppermost at any given time, all toddlers are relieved when the situation is calmly contained and resolved—when the angry child is stopped without meeting with an angry response, when they are assured that a teacher is likewise helping the overheard angry older preschooler, when the fly or bug is gently picked up and put outdoors. Likewise, they are reassured when damage to material is repaired and they learn that, in most instances, it had not been deliberately inflicted; when the mother who spoke harshly calms down and apologizes; when they are, once again, sure that Toddler Group is a safe place. Even the child who may have excitedly exhorted us to "Kill the bug! Kill it!" or who may have responded to a peer's angry outburst or action by initiating his own, shows instant relief in spite of a little grumble.

This is no doubt a measure of the extent of the toddler's fear of aggression, a fear which stems primarily from their self's weakness vis-à-vis the raw force of their own aggression and the real and imaginary damage it could cause. This fear is not in proportion to the child's manifest aggressive behavior. Many toddlers show little overt aggression. Many use extensive and rather effective means of keeping it out of their behavior and out of their consciousness. Temper tantrums are by no means the proverbial order of the day, and quite a few children have none or have them rarely and in very minor form. The children who do behave very aggressively usually do so at least in part for defensive reasons, as a means of warding off other feelings. As mentioned earlier (chapter 2), some of our toddlers had been very aggressive to peers in groups they had previously attended or at home with siblings. This subsided very quickly when their fear was pointed out and they were assured that everyone would be kept safe. It is not necessarily the overt quantity of aggression that engenders so much anxiety, but its nature, and the lack of reliable self-control. In the Toddler Group, where the children soon learn to rely on the adults' ability to be masters of their own aggression, and to protect the children from theirs, these inner struggles could be well observed.

AGGRESSION TO THE MOTHER

The most striking area of aggression can be seen in the love–hate impulses of the mother–child relationship. This often manifested itself in the form of a loyalty conflict.

> Ellen, barely 2 years old, was not physically aggressive but she often hurt her mother's feelings by disregarding mother's suggestions for activities or doing the opposite. When mother helped her with a puzzle of playdough shapes, Ellen often angrily messed up mother's work. For the most part, Ellen was similarly contrary with the teachers, but one day at snack time she suddenly addressed me as "Mommy." When the seeming error was pointed out, she replied, "But I want you to be my mommy." Her mother interjected in a hurt tone, "But what about me?" to which Ellen responded with "You can be the teacher."
>
> We explained, of course, that mommies always remain mommies, even when children sometimes wish it differently, that there was a lot of love between Ellen and her mommy, and she would soon learn that she can like a teacher as well. During the next few class sessions Ellen stayed very close to her mother and rejected us, barely said hello, refused help, and would not let us look at her work. On one such standoffish day she suddenly darted across the room and hugged and kissed me, glancing back at her mother in a triumphant way. This led to approaching the fact that her conflict was not around loving two people but over her intense anger at her mother.

Tom, at 18 months, clung to his mother and refused even to look at us, much less greet us. Although he used the toys and participated in the routines and activities, he looked solemn and acted as though we were not there. At home he happily told of all the nice songs he had learned and the toys he had played with. His mother felt comfortable with us and wanted him to be friendly, but he ignored her encouragement as he ignored us. This began to change only when we began to tell mother in front of him that sometimes children worry that if they liked us and wanted to do things with us there would not be enough love left for Mom and she might even leave them with us. Mother had not thought of that but, in the treatment-via-the-parent, she realized that at home she did in fact leave—to do some work, to go on an errand, or walk the dog—when father was at home and available to care for Tom. The parents had thought it appropriate and nice for Tom to have each of them to himself in turn, but as they started to explore Tom's feelings about this they learned that he viewed the changeover in terms of mutual rejection.

As discussed before (chapter 4), the toddlers who had experienced double or substitute care with father, grandmother, or housekeepers encountered heightened difficulty with mixed feelings, especially when the adults had not been aware of their charges' feelings about the arrangement. Whereas in Toddler Group the children's anger and concern about wishing to change caretakers surfaced in their loyalty conflict between mother and teachers, at home they usually did not protest or, as we could see during fathers' visits, often gleefully rejected mother while claiming him in an exaggerated way as their favorite.

However, the children's difficulty with tempering their aggression to the loved one focused on many circumstances and events, even without double or substitute parenting, and their struggles with it took many forms, apart from loyalty conflicts.

Carla, 22-months-old, had by and large managed to protect her mother from her anger, reinforcing her love with lots of affection, and by criticizing peers' angry behavior. Her continuing wetting and soiling contained some anger, but neither she nor mother were as yet aware of this. One day, during seemingly peaceful investigative play with the workbench tools, Carla suddenly picked up the wooden hammer and brought it forcefully to within an inch of mother's face, saying, "And we don't smash mommy's face with it." The shocked mother collected herself enough to join me in agreeing that hammers are not for hurting people and adding that they are not even for nearly hurting people. Angry feelings can be told and hammers are for pounding in pegs. But Carla could not trust herself to pound in pegs until some weeks later, when she had been helped to feel more in charge of her anger.

Some youngsters showed their aggression in struggles over bodily care, some in mauling, pushing at, and biting mother, even in the midst of what started out as hugging and cuddling; some mistreated her clothes or belongings or angrily threw and messed up the materials they were using with her. Anger at mother often took the form of being unkind to themselves and their things, as in messing themselves, spoiling what they had made, or disregarding safety rules to spite her. A few toddlers screamed in her face in ear-splitting fashion, and/or lost control, hitting and pummeling at her.

At times the children's aggression surfaced unprovoked, at times in response to frustration, but the extent of anger rarely matched its immediate cause. They realized or at least sensed the intense raw aggression in themselves, their intent to be rid of mother, to reject or exchange her, to "smash her face" or otherwise harm her. And it frightened them not only because they might expect retaliation in kind but because it eradicated their love. They gained very limited relief from mother's assurance that she still loved them, that it was all right to love daddy and to like the teachers, and that she would not do angry things back to them. What they really wanted to hear and yet could not believe was that *they* would still have loving feelings for mother and would succeed in not getting so angry because they loved her. "But I am always angry," said one boy with chagrin. Another questioned mother's "I love you even when I am angry at you," and whispered wide-eyed, "But I don't." It helped most when we acknowledged that it was scary to get so angry, and that it was indeed hard for them to feel love at these times, but that this gets easier as one grows bigger.

Soon they too will feel sure of always having loving feelings and their anger won't feel so big.

Several toddlers protected themselves and mother from mutual aggression by "giving" it to inanimate objects which they then feared, especially to noisy things, such as thunder, garbage trucks, sirens, helicopters, vacuum cleaners, and motorcycles. These fears usually subside as the child learns that, "These things make a big noise but they are not angry," and at the same time, is helped to gain better mastery of his aggression.

Although the toddler's aggression spares nobody, its main focus always is the mother. Other members of the family, well-liked outsiders, and peers do not merit that much anger (unless they serve as displacements from the mother), nor does anger at them cause as much fear or concern.

MANIFESTATIONS OF THE PLEASURE IN HURTING

In contrast to the fear of unadulterated aggression and concern over it, the toddlers tend to enjoy their sadistic ("hurting fun") impulses and behavior, and only begin to feel conflicted about it as they master the "turnaround" of these impulses into feelings of pity.

> One day a fledgling hopped around in our playground while the mother cardinal fluttered cooing around the fence. We told the children about this, prepared them for not using the area during our outside time, and promised they could watch the mother and baby from a specified distance. When the time came, Alan dashed outside ahead of his mother and rushed at the little bird with shooing motions, loud yells, and a gleeful grin. I managed to catch up with him but he made two more attempts. While Alan's sadistic forays went on, all the children watched him, his mother, and me, fascinated and with various degrees of vicarious pleasure. Only when he was safely in control without having been sadistically treated by the adults, did the others watch the birds and eventually speak disapprovingly of Alan having been "mean." Lest this become a chance for them to enjoy hurting his feelings, we agreed that Alan had shown he had trouble with "hurting fun" but added that he also wanted to be a kind boy and his mommy would help him.

Many toddlers viewed things on the ground as an invitation to sadistic stomping—ants, worms, mushrooms, weeds, not to mention mud, puddles, and icicles. Many wanted us to squash, spray, or kill the tiniest bug found indoors. Some showed beginnings of pity at the same time.

> At a little over 2 years old, Leonard was sincerely upset on finding a dead rabbit ("Poor little thing!") and insisted on burying it carefully with his mother. He was kind with little bugs in Toddler Group too. Yet over the next few months he occasionally caused unexpected "accidents." When it was his turn to look at a nest with a few fragile bird eggshells, he suddenly poked at them and reduced them to shattered bits. When he was carefully handed a tiny plant in a pot, he suddenly dropped the pot. It broke and damaged the plant. When I questioned the accidental nature of these mishaps, pointing out his momentary gleeful look, he had a shame-faced sheepish smile.

But most often, though usually subtly, the children enjoyed teasing their mothers and provoking them to join in the game. They were incredibly inventive in their many forms of minor torture and always cleverly targeted her weaknesses.

In contrast to the fun in hurting, the fun in being hurt was much less in evidence and was also not contained in the children's fantasies or symbolic play at home or in Toddler Group. Even in the provocations of mother to engage in teasing interactions, such as running off to be chased, the visible glee of upsetting her was much more pronounced than the pleasure in being caught. The few youngsters who had suffered much pain with medical–surgical treatments showed heightened sadistic fantasies, later interwoven with more extreme pity, but no attachment to or preoccupation with pain, either in response to hurts or in fantasy or play. Of the children who had been intermittently spanked, but not to the extent of being abused, one little girl showed pronounced pleasure in hurting as well as wishes to be hurt.

> Martha attended Toddler Group during her third year. Apart from being older than most of the others, she was also very verbal and competent. In spite of her many struggles with her

mother, she was a well-invested child in a close-knit family. Martha's intense excitement with her father and brother had escaped parental notice until she began to attend Toddler Group. There was much tussling, roughhousing, and boisterously affectionate body contact at home. Overstimulated, Martha would then "act up," couldn't sit still, couldn't settle down to sleep. These behaviors led to father's spankings, followed by tears and temporary peace. With increased awareness of Martha's anger, the parents toned down the daily excitements and discontinued spanking. At this point Martha's "asking for it" became evident. One day in Toddler Group, after once again succeeding in getting spanked by father, Martha danced in a flirtatious hip-swishing manner and sang along rhythmically "and then he'll spank the butt" with a coy smile. Asked about it, she first feigned angry complaint about father but then acknowledged that it was also fun.

THE PARENTS' AGGRESSION

None of the parents were deliberately, sadistically, righteously, or thoughtlessly aggressive. None of them used physical punishment as a regular or preferred means of discipline. Insofar as they yelled, threatened, spanked, or otherwise lost their temper, they felt more or less bad about it, even before their contact with the Hanna Perkins School. They often did not know how their behavior affected their child, but they generally knew how his affected them, namely that the toddler's disobedience, teasing, and lack of impulse control provoked them to the point of exasperation and utter helplessness at times: "I couldn't help myself"; "I didn't know what else to do"; "I had to show him who is boss." They had come to parenting with their own varied measure of difficulties in coping with anger, and when the child's behavior threatened or weakened their self-control they sometimes acted like toddlers themselves.

The children felt very threatened by parental aggression, regardless of whether it was directed at them or observed in interaction with others. They feared what could be done to them and worried about their own anger and trouble mastering it. Parental aggression accentuates the child's aggression. Instead of being able to look to the parental example as a hope and incentive toward achieving self-control, it suggests that as you get bigger your anger gets bigger and more dangerous. At the same time there is the implied loss of love, from the parent and for the parent, and the interference with loving self-investment of his body. The threat is so great that the toddlers do not protest or complain about the parents' outbursts unless or until they know and feel that the parents regret their behavior, try to tame their anger, and to understand and help the children with theirs. This then is the time when we start hearing about it in Toddler Group.

> Carla, whose wish to "smash mommy's face" was described above, had not been the target of her mother's anger, but her older sister had been, and Carla had also witnessed loud arguments between the parents. After mother had begun to help her hitherto rather quiet and compliant little daughter with anger and to deal better with her own, the following incident took place in Toddler Group.
> Carla had evidently become furious at her mother when the latter insisted that Carla put away one toy before getting out another. Carla's posture turned rigid, her face clouded over, and she pierced mother with a look that could kill. Then she quickly cuddled up to her and patted her arm with intrusive affection. When mother pointed out Carla's anger, Carla denied it. When I added that sometimes getting so angry at mom worries a girl and makes her want to have only loving feelings, Carla looked wide-eyed. Mother reassured her: "I still love you even when you get angry," to which Carla replied, "But when you yelled this morning you didn't have any love." Mother then took Carla in her arms, apologized for her trouble with yelling, and said she knew and was sorry it scared Carla and she, mother, was trying hard to do better. Carla looked somewhat relieved but insisted, "But you don't love me when you get angry." Mother's assurance on that score seemed to have left Carla disbelieving and puzzled. I then wondered with mother whether perhaps Carla, like most others her age, could not believe that anybody keeps on loving when angry because she herself can't do it. Carla nodded solemnly. Mother then picked up on this and told Carla that her loving feelings would always come back, she'll learn to keep them even when angry, just as mommy does, in spite of her trouble. At this Carla gave her mom a genuine hug and put away the toy.

The toddlers react to the parent's lack of protection from the aggression of others as though the parent had sanctioned the attack. There is often a kernel of truth to that, especially when the parent repeatedly exposes them to the same danger, repeatedly fails to intervene, disregards or minimizes the child's complaints or sustained hurts, or does not inquire sufficiently into what transpires during her absence.

> Adam, not yet 2 years old, often had scratches on his arms, but never showed them or complained, and when we noticed, sympathized, and inquired, he was quiet and changed the topic. Mother was sometimes surprised when we drew her attention, sometimes blamed his sister, but added that he had not told her about the hurts at the time. By contrast, in Toddler Group Adam was very upset at the least little hurt, and would even yell or lash out at peers when he thought they came too close to him. As mother began to show more concern about his scratches and why she didn't hear from him about them, and as we increasingly pointed out the defensive nature of his aggressive behavior and underlying fearfulness, Adam started to play baby-sitter with the dolls. The dolls hit each other and the sitter was angry, and sat them in the corner. It turned out that mother indeed left Adam too much at the sitter's mercy, but that he was also often attacked by bigger boys at the sitter's. The mother had not received any complaints from the sitter and assumed all went well. She had upheld the sitter as a nice woman, and attributed Adam's reluctance to go there to his anger at her going out without him. Once mother's denial ceased, she intervened and apologized to Adam. He began to alert mother and us to hurts sustained at home, and was less afraid and kinder with his peers. But his inner struggle with his anger continued and was much harder for him to resolve.

MASTERING AGGRESSION

Aggressive energy contributes a great deal to personality functioning and growth. Learning to use it in these ways is one of the developmental tasks of the toddler phase, one in which the parents and their relationship with the child play a crucial role.

Enjoyment of hurting and the behavior it prompts are the least adaptive aspects of aggression in our society. They are therefore most helpful and enriching when they are transformed—turned around—into pity, such as wanting to soothe and repair hurts. As with cleanliness, pity has the best chance of becoming a reliably maintained attribute and lasting part of the self-ideal when it is based on an identification with the loved, admired parents. In contrast to learning to like oneself clean, coming to feel pity does not allow for intermediate steps. There is no equivalent for the pleasurable water play in the tub or sink, for the anal–urinary gratification which, at least early on, is so much a part of cleaning, or for the painting, sandplay, or gardening which provide for the use of messy materials even when the process and goal have to be relatively neutral. Fixing, repairing, or "making better" are interfered with by the least admixture of fun in hurting, and making up after inflicting hurt is at best a temporary substitute for a true feeling of pity.

Yet the pleasure in hurting, like the pleasure in messing, are not just spontaneous, they are also readily evoked and intensified by the toddler's perception of an experience with them in his environment. The Toddler Group's educational approach to these matters was detailed earlier (chapter 2), but the parental attitudes, reflected in verbalizations and behavior as well as in the handling of those of the child, are the deciding factors. The parents we work with generally recognize and regret their own occasional pleasurable satisfaction in angry outbursts and are troubled by the primitive impulses their toddlers provoke in them, even when these impulses remain wishes and thoughts and are not acted on. The parents are much less aware of the many daily practices and events which they accept habitually, but which their toddler newly perceives in their basic form. Among these are not only the already mentioned killing of insects and worms (so different from essential pest control), but the hitting or other mistreatment of pets, and eating meat, which often prompts inquiries at dinner ("Was that a chicken? Who killed it?"). Children will see stuffed animals in a museum or mounted antlers in someone's living room, learn about fishing and hunting as a sport, and the preparation of carcasses, TV programs and the news deal with sadistic matters, and many adults, including fathers, tease children and are often quite oblivious to its effect on them. As parents begin to look at these incidents with their toddler's eyes, they often start to rethink and reevaluate what they had taken for granted and to differentiate necessary hurts from those prompted by enjoyment or disregard. More often than not, toddlers also perceive medical and surgical treatments as sadistic. Some parents explain that the doctor's job is to make people better or to keep them healthy, that he has learned to do it in the kindest and best way, and is sorry when it hurts people. Others focus on an intellectual explanation of all the instruments and how they are used, without realizing that too much information cannot be absorbed and appeals to the sadism instead. Still others threaten the child with the hospital to make him follow safety rules or swallow medicine. Parents do not have to be perfect, but it helps a great deal when they are in touch with their own and their toddler's impulses and are able to contain them.

Displacement of aggression, diverting aggression to a substitute target, is often advocated as a helpful discharge and as a stepping stone toward developing interests which utilize active energy, such as woodwork or sports. Our negative experience with these educational measures in the work with older youngsters was confirmed by the observation of toddlers. Hitting the punching bag when angry at mother does not help the child to tame his anger. Instead it tends to pave the way for other, less adaptive, displacements. Given the toddler's difficulty in distinguishing animate from inanimate, and lack of appreciation of others' feelings, it sometimes, as we have seen, contributes to the idea: "Hurt those that can't or won't hurt you back." Also, maltreating things is not usually acceptable to the adults and quite frightening for the child. A truly maltreated punching bag may get damaged or destroyed; furniture, toys, and walls certainly do. Nor do these displacements help to channel and transform aggression.

Alan, 2 years old, had been permitted much scope for displacement. Full of untrammeled boisterous energy he rammed his tricycle into posts and doors, practiced his punches on anything that happened by, and bashed vigorously at the workbench.

When angry and frustrated, he threw the blocks or scattered the puzzle pieces and tore the drawing paper. Some of this behavior stemmed from his fear of the aggression of others, but it also contributed to his fear of his own aggression and did not in the least help him to learn skills. He felt better as soon as our "everybody and everything has to be safe" rule was spelled out and enforced, with only verbal expression permitted. I then asked him if he would like to learn to handle the hammer properly, the way people really use a hammer. He agreed, and we embarked on many practicing sessions. When he had to direct the blow carefully to hit the peg, Alan was at first quite clumsy and hesitant, but his aim improved, he began to use more purposeful strength, and was delighted when he could really do it. We went on to learning to use the hammer to pull out the pegs. It was a much harder task, requiring both more strength and more skill and it took some time to master. The first success even toppled him over backwards and more practice was necessary to focus his energy solely in his arm. In time Alan became a skillful and zestful worker with tools and other activities. Whereas the earlier displacements had provided impulse gratification and caused him to worry, now his pleasure derived largely from mastery with the help of transformed and channeled energy.

The developing personality functions, such as motor control, have to be invested with both pleasure-seeking and aggressive urges, but cannot serve as means of discharge and direct impulse gratification. Parents and educators facilitate the process of transforming and channeling the energy of the urges by curbing the opportunities for direct impulse gratification, by making mastery pleasurable, and by providing many opportunities for building and exercising skills in the context of a supportive relationship. The relationship itself is a prime vehicle for learning to tame aggression.

Taming aggression for the sake of love is the part of the overall task of mastery which the toddler himself wants most. He wants it out of fear of his own and the parents' aggression but, if he is to succeed, he also wants it out of love and admiration for the parents whom he wishes to emulate. Such an identification forms the basis for the many attributes and values which make it possible to maintain close and lasting relationships, to be considerate of others, and to respect life in all forms.

Taming aggression in this sense is not achieved via verbalization, although the step from physical to verbal expression is very important and we take for granted educational measures to foster it. It also is not achieved by helping the child to differentiate thoughts and wishes from action, although this too is very important in reducing the fear of aggression and in giving it harmless scope. Taming aggression consists primarily of love binding aggression and thereby rendering it less dangerous, as well as transforming it into useful active energy. Such taming of aggression for the sake of love succeeds only when there is more love than anger in the mutual relationship. As already illustrated in some of the above cases and in the description of our educational approach (chapter 2), the children are helped by being reminded of their loving feelings at times of anger so that, like the mother, they can use them to preserve her and the mutually loving relationship with her. Recognizing that we have love along with anger, helps us to want to spare the loved one but it also involves some inner conflict.

> When Justin's mother planned to take a brief and necessary trip out of town, he was furious with her. At first this showed indirectly in his disgruntled manner and contrary behavior, then it surfaced in his rejection of her help in setting up the paints for him and insisting that the teacher do it. When it was pointed out that he seemed very angry at Mom, so angry that he wouldn't have anything to do with her and wanted the teacher instead, he burst out, "She's a bad mommy. I hate her." While mother linked Justin's anger to her trip and assured him she still loved him, the teacher reminded him that he also still loved his mother, that just the other day he had talked of their good time baking cookies. Everyone gets angry at their mom sometimes but it feels better to remember also the "good mom." Actually, Justin did not feel better right away. He looked conflicted and just stood there quietly. He did not resist mother equally quietly readying the paints. By the time he had finished using them, they gave each other a nice hug.

The parental valuing of the child's effort at restraint helps to increase his love, through being loved and appreciated and through feeling good about himself. When a toddler succeeds in using his love to tame his aggression, there is enormous relief and good feeling. They reflect a sense of inner mastery which is quite different from stopping his angry behavior to avoid the mother's punitive anger or just to please her. As this inner mastery gets under way, the child is not merely better behaved. He is much more at peace with himself, has much more available energy for play and activities, and more confidence in his abilities. Above all, there is a marked increase in overall pleasure, including pleasure in need-fulfillment, in social interactions, in doing things, and interest in the world around him. And it helps him to feel and be a really put-together person. Mothers' comments usually address this: "He's got it all together, so he's happy now"; "Isn't it great to see her so 'with it'!" "She's just enjoying life these days." Increase in pleasure, in feeling good, and in overall personality integration were the most marked and most frequent improvements noted in the end-of-year Toddler Group Achievement Summary. On the mother's side they correlated with the extent to which she had got in tune with her child, on his side they invariably correlated with taming of aggression and freeing its energy for personality use.

It is never an all or none achievement, and later developmental stresses put it to a test. But the children who did achieve a substantial measure of success in taming their aggression fared much better and faced a less difficult task than those who did not.

Many circumstances contribute to heightened difficulty with taming aggression, some of which have already been described. Typically those children who had problems with aggression had experienced double parenting or extensive substitute parenting without being helped to recognize and deal with their feelings about the unavailable parent, and the need for the repeated change of caretaker. The persistence of unresolved aggressive mouth impulses from infancy and the experiences relating to this was another factor. Marked evidence of difficulty with aggression in the mother and in her relationship with the child was also significant. In these and, no doubt, many other situations the difficulty appeared primarily related to an excessive stimulation of anger. Then there were the difficulties of those toddlers who lacked sufficient opportunities for loving and being loved. Among the toddlers we worked with this applied in cases where one parent was absent or partially absent through marital separation or divorce. As described with Debbie (chapter 4) and Carole (chapter 8), these children needed to have their own love for their father confirmed and accepted, benefited greatly from being assured that he had some good qualities and love for them, even when his troubles interfered, and were especially helped when a measure of satisfying contact with the father could be reestablished. We were repeatedly astonished by the extent to which an even very limited increase in loving and being loved favorably affected the balance between love and anger and thereby contributed to the ability to tame aggression. Much greater difficulty with taming aggression was evident in some children who had experienced earlier traumatic overwhelming—through abuse or medical–surgical treatments. The overwhelming had incapacitated their personality's means of coping while, at the same time, causing gross overstimulation of excited and aggressive urges.

Regardless of the nature or degree of difficulty in mastering aggression, and regardless of the factors which contributed to it, all the children nevertheless showed evidence of pleasure-seeking and aggressive urges. This was quite different with Marjorie. Our experiences with her underlined just how important urges are for growth and life itself.

Marjorie had suffered so much illness and neglect from birth on that she was medically diagnosed as failure-to-thrive in the latter part of her second year. At this time she came under the permanent care of a dedicated, loving foster mother. Marjorie made a good bodily recovery and formed a close attachment to her second mother. She achieved age-appropriate self-care, showed competent functions and skills, used the teachers well, observed all group rules without difficulty, and was interested in and respectful of her peers. But there was no or minimal affect. Her face was often blank, and there was neither excitement nor aggression. She initially did not even eat, much less enjoy eating, unless mother remained close by her and ate with her. She did not light up with praise for her good behavior or work, nor did she appear pleased with herself.

For some time we wondered whether her behavior resulted from extreme self-control and strong defenses, motivated perhaps by fear of angry retaliation. There may have been a measure of that as we observe it often in children who gear all their energy to survival in a threatening environment. But Marjorie also used no self-comforting habits and no blankie or soft toy. Her doll was not used for play, and when asked about its name, she gave the commercial trade name. She was not accident prone and did not direct anger at herself in any form. When something hurt or she did not feel well, she was stoic, became more subdued, and accepted mother's comfort and care. We could only conclude that Marjorie's pleasure-seeking impulses had not been sufficiently stimulated and that her aggression had not been developmentally mobilized, and hence did not press for discharge. There appeared to have been some positive need-fulfilling and relationship experiences which had enabled her to survive, to respond to the foster mother's nurturing, and to promote functional development in her new home.

We were therefore very encouraged when Marjorie began to show excitement and real pleasure and became more rambunctious and less obedient. She was never physically aggressive but could look very angry, ignore people and requests in a purposefully rejecting way, and proceed determinedly with what she wanted to do. She came to enjoy her food more for herself, withheld bowel movements for a number of reasons, including some contrariness, and became rather show-offy, commanding center stage at circle time. She ran and skipped excitedly in the hall and urged on her mother in happy anticipation of entering our room, and sometimes, with sparkling eyes, would not stop chattering away.

In her later personality growth she encountered many inner and outer obstacles, many of them focused on her lack of available loving feelings and difficulty in dealing with her own and others' anger, often perceived in terms of rejection. But her urges continued to develop appropriately, she invested herself fully in her family threesome and found her place in it, and, later, became a proper schoolgirl. We felt that of all the help she received, the most crucial had been the building of the relationship with the foster mother which had helped her urges to "pick up" and fuel her development.

ANGER USED FOR SELF-DEFENSE

For a long time Marjorie had not been able to defend herself. She would give up her place and materials when others wanted them, and never appealed for help from the adults in these situations. Later on, in play with peers she had difficulty sticking up for her ideas, accepted others' bossiness, or withdrew hurt and stubbornly resisted offered assistance. Although it took her an especially long time to stand up for herself and her rights, all young children experience difficulty with learning to defend themselves appropriately and need much help (E. Furman, 1987). Many factors within the child's personality and in his relationships and experiences contribute. Among these the child's self-love and mastery of aggression stand out. Many toddlers feel helpless and afraid when their bodies, belongings, or rights are encroached upon, and they rely on the parent to intervene and protect them. From this feeling comes their frequent assumption that lack of protection implies that the parents allowed or even arranged the assault, and hence also the anxiety and confusion when the parent inflicts a hurt instead of protecting. Some toddlers, either because they have been encouraged to do so or out of fear, respond to infringement with vehement attack, and may even attack when they perceive or imagine that something might be done to them or to their things. Some use self-defense as a deliberate or defensive opportunity for indiscriminate aggressive discharge, while some very aggressive youngsters may become paralyzed, subdued, or bewildered in the face of being done to, angrily or unintentionally.

Becoming independently self-protective vis-à-vis others depends on the one hand on the very gradual internalization of the parents' valuing and protectiveness of the child, of his body, feelings, functions, achievements, and belongings. On the other hand, it requires accurate assessment of the reality and sufficient inner control so that the most appropriate form and amount of aggression will be used or that any aggressive response will be refrained from in favor of flight, and/or seeking help. The toddlers were therefore helped most by being protected, by being assured of the value and rights of each, and by being encouraged to use appropriate means of self-defense, with adult supervision, in those situations where minor infringements occurred. For example, a child has to learn how to hold onto a toy, how to object to someone invading his space. He has to learn how to demand appropriate repair or substitution when something of his gets damaged. He has to learn how to state firmly his dislike of a peer's unexpected or too strong hug, and insisting on the right to speak and to be heard without being interrupted. Bodily attacks are so frightening for toddlers that they need to rely on adult prevention or help in dealing with the situation, and cannot be expected to fend for themselves. "Hit him back when he hits you" is not good advice in all such situations. What if it leads to getting beaten up by a stronger or more aggressive opponent? Hitting back or even demolishing the attacker may be the best self-defense in some instances, but a child would have to be much older and more mature before he would be able to gauge such a reality correctly or have his aggression in sufficient self-control.

CHAPTER 8

Feelings

Young babies experience a variety of bodily sensations, some comfortable, some uncomfortable, and they respond to them in bodily ways—crying, screaming, smiling, kicking legs and waving arms, becoming relaxed, restless, or rigid, throwing up and having cramps or diarrhea, or digesting food peacefully. Gradually, and with mother's help, they begin to know and differentiate these sensations and to experience them in a mental form as feelings. Toddlerhood is the time when the transition from bodily sensations and discharge to awareness and owning of feelings is most striking. As the toddler progresses from tummy aches, hyperactive restlessness, or seemingly angry pushing and throwing of things, to knowing and bearing his anger, sadness, envy, happiness, and many other feelings, he is taking a major developmental step. The toddlers' pace of growth in this area varies enormously and depends significantly on the mother's role as facilitator. The sooner and the more reliably we know, experience, and differentiate feelings, the better they serve us to understand the situation which causes us to have a certain feeling and to gauge what to do about it. Getting there is not only a slow process but one never fully achieved. Even in adulthood, intense feelings are often accompanied by bodily responses, such as nausea or diarrhea with anger, upset, and fear, or "jumping for joy" with pleasure. But for the most part, older children and adults experience feelings in mental rather than bodily form.

FEELING GOOD AND NOT FEELING GOOD

As with so many early personality developments, learning to feel is initially linked to getting to know and like his body. The infant's first real feeling (as opposed to the earlier reflex crying in response to distress) is that of bodily discomfort or pain, and he uses it to protest and to seek and accept comfort. This major achievement is usually accomplished by the latter half of the first year and is linked to the related achievement of feeling good. Insofar as her baby is relatively normally endowed and spared the experience of protracted painful illness and treatments, the mother's role in helping him to experience both these basic feelings depends on two prerequisites (E. Furman, 1985b, 1991): (1) her own ability to feel bodily good and bad and to know, bear, and contain these feelings sufficiently so that she can use them to take appropriate steps in response; (2) the mother's ongoing loving investment of her infant. As has been detailed earlier (chapter 3), this investment has to include sufficient love of the child as a part of herself so that she is able to feel and do for him what she can feel and do for herself. That is to say, she needs to recognize and gather up the child's diverse sensations and discharges and give them feeling mental form and content with a name—"That feels good," "That feels bad." At the same time, mother's investment has to contain sufficient love for the child as a separate person so that she can recognize and appreciate his feelings when they are different from hers, and can value and support his knowing, bearing, and using of his feelings (not make them her own). When all aspects of these two prerequisites are available to a good-enough extent, the mother can feel with her child or, as we tend to say, she is "in tune." She is in a good position to embark on the intricate gradual steps of transferring to him her own appreciation and know-how regarding the possession and use of feelings, and of supporting his increasing ability to do so, while remaining in feeling touch, usually even after he has made this an integral part of his personality, independent of her.

Even though feeling bodily discomfort (and the response of protesting and seeking and accepting comfort) is the first feeling acquisition, it remains vulnerable. It is easily lost during the early years when mother is absent or emotionally unavailable. Toddlers in day care often fail to experience and protest pain, and recover their ability to do so only on reuniting with mother, or even not at all (E. Furman, 1984). Likewise, children separated from mother during a hospital stay are often "good" uncomplaining patients and show distress only when the mother visits; that is, when they recover their ability to feel. Feeling bodily pain also tends to be the last feeling to be used independently to initiate appropriate action, long after this has been achieved with many later feelings. Thus it is the rule, rather than the exception, for college-aged young men and women to call home first when they are ill, and only then to contact their local physician. In spite of this prolonged developmental process, the early achievements of feeling and protesting pain, and seeking and accepting mother's comfort, are not only crucial to survival but are the basis for the mother–child work on other feelings. In our Toddler Group we have therefore learned to pay close attention to the toddlers' and mothers' attitudes to bodily pain. We try to understand just which aspects facilitate or impede mastery, and to help educationally and therapeutically.

Chris, a healthy infant, had, from early on, suffered much discomfort from teething. At 18 months, and with the help of his mother, they related that morning's experience: Chris had called his mom, looked teary and unhappy, pointing with his finger inside and to the back left of his mouth, and reached out to her. She picked him up for a hug, told him she understood he had a toothache, and was sorry it hurt. He then took her to the refrigerator where he pointed out the bottle with a local analgesic they kept for relieving teething pain, and took part in applying it. They could both feel the bump. The medicine helped, but throughout the day Chris remained aware of his discomfort and alerted mom to it. She offered him a Tylenol she had brought along, and he took it. Mom sympathized and praised his choice of cold soft foods. She also told him how nice it was that he knew it didn't feel good, that the hurt was coming from a new tooth, that he could tell her, and find the right things to do for it. Although Chris was subdued, he maintained his usual good functioning.

Kent, also a healthy and loved infant, had suffered several strep throat infections. When he was over 2 years old, I noticed him one day as listless, irritable, poking his hand into the back of his mouth, yawning. I shared my observations with his mom. She was aware of them, added that he had not eaten well, and had woken during the night. She thought a tooth might be bothering him, but she had not talked with him about it, nor was she solicitous of his evident discomfort. I told her I thought Kent was not feeling well and had a sore throat. She disagreed, then suddenly and matter-of-factly asked him, "Does your throat hurt?" He resented the intrusion and pushed her away with an angry "No."

The next day Kent's functioning deteriorated further. He fell twice, screamed and kicked at the least frustration, messed with his snack. When Kent at one point coughed as if choking and grabbed at his neck, mother phoned the doctor at once, and rushed him off to be examined. Had I not interfered, she would not have stopped to explain all this to her boy and to prepare him. It was a very sore strep throat and Kent was put on antibiotics which mom administered conscientiously. She complained that he spat out his medicine and pushed away the squirter she used to insert it. I sympathized with mother and child about how hard it was not to feel good and not to be able to make oneself feel better and, since both of them wanted to make the throat better, perhaps Kent would like to suck the medicine off a spoon himself and mom might have a candy ready for afterwards, to help with the bad taste. This helped with the medicine and with the hard feelings between them. The mother's deep distress and hurt at having failed to diagnose the illness prompted her to work on this in the treatment-via-the-parent and this led her to a beginning appreciation of her child's feelings as well.

The mother–child attitudes to bodily pain tend to set a pattern which is often carried over to the development of other feelings, as illustrated by the case of Barbara.

After an earlier history of either not protesting pain at all or snuggling into mother helplessly overwhelmed, Barbara showed a similar all or none response with embarrassment and anger. At 2½, she appeared quite unconcerned over wetting and soiling which mother attributed to her "not being ready." But when Barbara spilled a little juice while pouring it from the pitcher into her cup, she felt mortified, cried helplessly, climbed into mom's lap, and buried herself into mother's enveloping arms, as mother kindly reassured her. When angry at mom, Barbara at times disintegrated into a temper tantrum, again pushing into mother who contained her in her arms, often telling Barbara and us that the child was just tired or had a bit of a cold.

But for the most part, Barbara did not show anger at all. When peers took her toys, she did not protest, and when they intruded on her play, she let them. Initially mother was pleased that Barbara "shared so well" and was "kind to others," but she came to appreciate our concern at Barbara's lack of self-defense. She related it to her own trouble with saying "no," taking on tasks that overburdened her, and ending up with everyone at each other in uncontrolled ways. Not wanting to pass on her difficulty to her child made her want to work on this. She acknowledged to Barbara her own trouble with anger and promised to help her so Barbara could do better. And Barbara soon did. She began to stand up for herself and even took the lead with mother. One day, when mom disapproved of Barbara's good painting of angry monsters, Barbara said, "But Mommy, it's only a picture." Another day, when mother again suggested that Barbara's angry defiance of a request was due to fatigue, the child yelled, "No, I'm not tired, I am angry." Mother agreed. With mother's support, despite her trouble, Barbara learned to have and use her own anger.

Embarrassment was harder for Barbara. Here mother had to help in a different way. She told Barbara that feeling ashamed for making a mess is hard for everyone, but that Barbara would feel better if she took care of the feeling and mess herself, instead of mommy doing it for her. With the next spill, Barbara crawled under the table. Mother pointed out that hiding away only makes others notice it more. She would feel better if she cleaned up and were more careful next time. Barbara did so with downcast eyes. In time she mastered not only pouring juice but using the toilet.

FEELING AND BEING FELT WITH

It may seem that Chris, Kent, and Barbara had simply taken over their mothers' feeling or lack of feelings and that this is the manner in which children develop feelings. It is not. Feeling what mother feels bypasses the development of the child's own feelings and results in a lasting inner confusion and uncertainty, sometimes covered by adopting other people's ways of showing feelings, but never enabling the child to use his feelings as a guide to assessing reality and then acting accordingly. When the toddler takes his cue about what to feel from his mother, she has actually failed to feel with him, has assumed that he would only feel what she feels, or, worse yet, what she wants him to feel. Truly feeling with implies assisting the child in crystallizing his own feelings and coming to know them with the help of his mother's validation and appreciation of them as his. He can then identify with her means of containing, differentiating, and using them, and verbalization is among those means. The examples of Mary and Martin illustrate the contrast.

> At 13 months, Mary was one day running around discontentedly, kicking at her toys, and ignoring mother's requests to join her for a snack. Mother watched for a while and then said, "Mary, you are angry at mommy." Mary stopped, looked at her mother bewildered, and questioning. "Yes, when you kick and run around and won't come with me and nothing feels right, that's when you are angry. It's okay. Everyone gets angry." Mary's face lit up with relief as if something suddenly made sense and fit together. She came to a halt, drew herself up tall, and repeated, "Angy, angy." "Yes, you can tell me you are angry," said her mother. The experience of understanding herself through being understood and having it all contained in a word, a symbol, provided so much pleasurable mastery that Mary even forgot about her anger. It returned later and could then be linked to its cause, mother going out and leaving her with her sitter.

> Martin, also 13 months old, was put in a day care home with several other, mostly older, toddlers, while his mother started

back to work half-days. Mother would return to pick up Martin in the early afternoons, arriving with a happy face and jolly talk about how glad she was that Martin had had such a fun time with all the kids and toys, and there were excited hugs before driving home. Martin usually fell asleep en route and then had his bottle at home. By age 2 years, Martin responded not only to separations but to all feeling situations with excited behavior and a rather strained happy grin. The seemingly happy excitement would soon turn rambunctious, aggressive, and destructive, but Martin was unable to recognize this and claimed he was happy and having fun. Mother's anger at his behavior only increased the excitement as well as the mutual barrier against feeling and feeling with.

When toddlers have not been helped to make mental sense of their sensations and discharges and to know and value their own feelings, they may adopt mother's feeling responses, but they may simply persist with bodily manifestations. This is not only a natural consequence of having failed to make the transition to feelings, but is often supported by mothers. As with Barbara, described above, many mothers relate the children's behavior to bodily needs instead of mental feelings—"You are just tired"; "You're getting hungry"; "You have a cold coming." At best, the transition from body to mind takes a long time. It is almost impossible for a toddler to feel and say he is happy without jumping up and down or dancing around, to feel and say he is angry without mean scowls, raised voice, and a forceful forward leaning posture, or to feel and say he is sad without cuddling into an embrace.

Some children who are not felt with and remain at the mercy of their overwhelming sensations may use a variety of primitive means of coping.

Two-year-old Alan fought the world. His screaming and running ahead of his mother could be heard from the hall. When he entered our room he barged around from toy to toy, handling them roughly, snatching things from others, angrily denying every request, often hitting out or teasily running off and throwing things. He was unable to sit at snack where he tried to poke into mother or at others and disrupted our songs with his noise and aggressive hyperactivity. His mother's constant verbal directions went unheeded and, as often as he could, he wrenched away from her bodily hold on him. Everyone felt intimidated, and this provided the first clue: I assured Alan this was a safe place and that neither he nor others could be hurt. And I enforced this, calmly but firmly. Although he had no understandable speech, he began to make eye contact with me and relaxed somewhat. I then noticed that, just before his sudden bouts of hollering and acting up, there would be a moment when he looked scared. This I verbalized sympathetically and encouraged him to show us what was scary. Finally one day he pointed to the ceiling. With effort, I could make out the slight noise of a toilet flushing on the second floor. He was much relieved that I understood, explained, and declared it safe. When I had initially shared my observation with mother, she could not believe that her tough boy was ever scared, but she became more receptive and supporting of Alan as, day by day, we learned of more fears—noises, changes, visitors, fears of being sent way, of being stupid, helpless, and incompetent. Being felt with, he could increasingly feel his scares and use his feeling to help himself, sometimes to seek explanation, sometimes to learn to master an activity, or to modify his behavior. He also became softer, could experience pleasure, and show loving feelings. He became a person.

Unlike Alan, many even younger toddlers are well able to experience a variety of feelings. But they cannot trust and accept them and cannot feel they themselves are acceptable, when mother does not feel with them. They then ward off their feelings and are no longer aware of them, but above all, we observe poor bodily and mental self-regard, lack of trust in themselves and the world around them, and increased dependence on mother.

Two-year-old Carole clung to her mother and was standoffish with the teachers. She chose very easy activities to do privately with mother, but never seemed pleased with her accomplishments. When a teacher approached or asked to look at her work, she crossly refused and hid it away. Yet she herself keenly observed everyone and tried to attract admiration by wearing bows and jewelry. Mother was surprised when we pointed out Carole's evident loyalty conflict, but she considered this and assured Carole that it was all right to like the teachers and that there would still be lots of love left between mommy and Carole. This helped the relationships but not Carole's liking of herself.

Father had left the family several months earlier after protracted marital discord and some abusive outbursts at the mother and Carole's older brother. Visits with father were more or less weekly, but Carole never mentioned him, nor did mother. When other fathers visited Toddler Group, Carole was subdued, with pained sidelong glances at the dads and increased closeness to mother. We alerted the mother to this so that she could support us when, at the next opportunity, I quietly told Carole and mom, "A girl might miss her own daddy and wish he could be with her too, like the other daddy. That's hard, but a dad can still like his girl and be a very nice dad, even if he can't come to visit." On their way home the dam broke. Carole was furious at mom, blaming her for "kicking out" daddy, whom she loved, who was so nice, and with whom she wanted to live. In her rage she even threw out her own beloved teddy which mother retrieved. Having been prepared by the therapist and teachers, mother could begin to feel with Carole, apologize for not having understood, and help her. Mother confessed that she had not believed us because she simply could not imagine that Carole's feelings about the father were so different from her own. Mother's new empathy and appreciation of Carole's feelings led to much improvement in her daughter's strides in bodily self-care, zest, and pleasure in activities, as well as kindness with mother, teachers, and peers. She even happily showed off gifts from her dad.

We see a similar marked increase in self-esteem even in cases where the feelings relate to daily events and ordinary developmental concerns. The enhanced self-esteem appears to result from the comprehension, validation, and integration of what had been a vague inner turmoil, experienced as bewildering and deemed strange and unacceptable.

Two-year-old Hank's parents had wanted him to be a perfectly happy child. They had done their best to bring this about, and fate had cooperated by introducing no unavoidable hardships. Hank had cooperated too by not becoming aware of his unhappy feelings about himself. Not being felt with made these feelings and indeed all of himself seem unacceptable, and this further diminished his self-regard. His only way out was to put everything he did not like about himself onto others and in this way remain perfectly fine in his own and in his parents' eyes. He was so out of touch with his feelings that he could not even communicate with others. Instead of listening and responding to a question, he imagined a potential criticism and turned defensive; when asked about his new truck, he replied crossly, "I didn't have to make a picture." Sometimes these "replies" left us feeling stupid and put off, just as Hank no doubt often felt without knowing it. Sometimes we could follow his association. In this instance with the picture he appeared to refer to his adamant refusals to engage in activities. He did not know that he was avoiding activities because he feared showing up badly or having his work compare poorly with that of others. He merely viewed his refusals as rejecting us and what we could offer. He also made his peers feel stupid, little, and unacceptable with his critical and denigrating remarks and rejection of their invitations to play. The more he avoided not-liking-himself feelings, the less likable he made himself. Interestingly, he focused his rebuffs and insults especially on a boy who, though troubled in some ways, had an unusual ability to feel his emotions intensely and who was therefore in feeling touch with himself and with everyone else.

It was very painful for the parents to realize that Hank was not really happy. Mother began to wonder with him whether perhaps he thought others were so stupid and not worth playing with because he sometimes felt that way about himself. She assured him that it was okay to feel that way, that they could think together about the reasons for his feelings, and see how he could help himself to feel better. Hank soon let his mom know. He could not ride his tricycle as well as others, could not paint nice pictures, dirtied his pants, was left out of mom's and dad's evenings, felt envious and mean and didn't like himself for that. One evening mother and child had a long talk about all this. Mother was thrilled that she could actually talk *with* Hank, and he seemed a much more zestful, outgoing, and indeed happy boy almost right away. There was much work to be done, however, and Hank did not always find it easy. Yet, in spite of setbacks, there had been a turning point. Having had his feelings accepted, he could accept himself better.

Carole and Hank were no doubt close to being aware of at least some of their feelings. Others are not. A child may act very aggressively without knowing he is angry, and tears may roll down his cheeks without his feeling sad. Many children wet in lieu of crying. The bodily discharge is not necessarily specific, and its feeling equivalent may be as unrecognizable to the adult as it is to the child. Bodily discharge may be used as a defense against feelings when the parents are unable to feel with the child and support his tolerance and use of them.

OWNING AND USING FEELINGS

In many ways the child's learning to own and use his feelings proceeds through the same four stages in interaction with the mother as were described regarding mastery of bodily self-care (chapter 3)—doing for, doing with, standing by to admire, and independent functioning. With feelings, however, there are also some differences for mother and child.

The initial achievement of feeling and being felt with provides a markedly pleasurable mastery and relief, especially as the mother helps to contain the feeling and, more often than not, relieves it by relating it to the appropriate realities and taking steps to ameliorate the situation. When little Mary was angry, mother linked it to her leaving, encouraged Mary to express her anger in words, no doubt assured her of continuing love and speedy return, and probably offered Mary something of mother's to keep and/or a little gift on coming back. When Carole was sad about missing her father, mother comforted her and facilitated visits with father. In Toddler Group, envy of another's birthday is not only recognized and sympathized with but mitigated by being given a little "favor," as well as the promise of a later celebration for the child.

The subsequent steps in mastering feelings are harder. Learning to care for his body always leads to a good feeling in the end, in spite of the child's frustrations with failure along the way, and in spite of mother's frustrations with helping him and having to adapt her relationship with him. Learning to own and use his feelings does not always entail a happy ending.

Learning to link the feeling to the appropriate situation is at times more difficult for the mother; for example, when the child is angry at mom; when mom is to blame for his distress; when she wants to protect her own feelings by "sparing" him from hard feelings; or when his feelings in a situation are very different from her own, as was the case with Carole and as is often the case with divorce. At other times it is more difficult for the child, especially when he fears the intensity of his feelings and their consequences. It seems always safer to be angry at a younger sibling than at the parent, and it is always less painful to blame mother for not getting the puzzle right than to blame oneself for not knowing how to fit it together. Both for different and shared reasons, mother and child shy away from acknowledging the appropriate reality.

Likewise, it is often difficult for either or both of them to accept the fact that some realities cannot be changed, perhaps can barely be alleviated, and the feeling still has to be experienced and contained. There are not only major unalterable realities, such as bereavements, illnesses, and bodily handicaps, but many daily and developmental ones. Mother may need to go to work, or a child may wish to be adult, or there may be a little thing such as Toddler Group ending at 11 o'clock in the midst of an enjoyable playtime. At all these times, helplessness as well as other feelings can threaten to get "too big," may feel overwhelming, may press for bodily and motoric discharge, or may just leave one thoroughly miserable. Many mothers and all children do not appreciate the value and importance of feelings in these situations and avoid or ward them off.

But owning and using feelings cannot be arbitrarily restricted to certain feelings in certain situations. Invariably, avoidance and defense used in one set of circumstances spread to others and/or interfere with the whole developmental process of mastery. It is essential therefore to value the ability to feel as such and to value the use of feelings in assessing and coping with inner and outer realities, even when they only enable us to know that we cannot do anything about these realities. Just as we still keep and cherish our arms when they are sore and stiff, so we need to value our ability to feel pleasurable as well as unpleasurable emotions. In the Toddler Group we have many opportunities to assist mothers and toddlers in this process. For example, when a child is sad, disappointed, unhappy, we always support mothers in conveying how grown-up it is to let himself have such a hard feeling, and we often add that when we are able to have big hard feelings we can also have big good feelings. Practicing the necessary endurance and self-control does not come easily. It requires a lot of parental support and investment as well as example, and above all, feeling with. The child can only learn to tolerate and contain feelings when the adult can bear them with him. The toddlers do not know yet that owning all their feelings makes for a rich emotional life, for empathy with others, and relating with them. Nor do they know how crucial a tool feelings are to an understanding of what is really going on inside us as well as in the world around us. But they do experience the heightened self-confidence and sense of mastery which are brought about by owning and using feelings as a part of one's self. When Barbara told her mother, "I'm not tired, I am angry," she was self-assuredly "all there." Nobody could resist admiring her. But a child who can feel intensely is not only respected, he is liked, by himself and others.

CHAPTER 9

The Development of Personality Tools

Personality tools (or functions) are the means we use to understand and cope with ourselves, with others, and with the world. Our tools include motor control (the coordinated use of small and large muscles), using words (speech), memory, perceiving with our senses, thinking, and interpreting correctly what goes on in our bodies and minds as well as in the world around us (i.e., knowing inner and outer reality). We use all these tools together, as our own, in such a way as to ensure that we can rely on their serving us at all times. As adults we take all this for granted. We don't even realize or appreciate how important these tools are for us and how much they add to our competence in daily living, self-confidence, and well-being. At times of illness, incapacitation, or in old age, when one or the other personality tool no longer serves us, we come closer to understanding how an infant or toddler feels before his functions have developed and, even as they begin to grow, what it takes before the child can truly count on them and use them. Many years of study—others' and our own—have shown us that health, endowment, and maturational unfolding are by no means the only factors leading to the development of personality functions. Attitudes within the child and the mother make important contributions and codetermine to what extent each

153

function will grow into a truly reliable serviceable tool and become fully integrated into the personality (E. Furman, 1987). It takes many steps over a long period of time.

THE NATURE OF THE MOTHER'S INVESTMENT

In the Toddler Group we tried, from the start, to observe closely the mother–child interactions in relation to the developing functions and the many behaviors which commonly demonstrate a mother's facilitating or impeding attitudes. These might include her ability to provide safety and opportunity for the exercise of these behaviors, to gauge the child's readiness so as to avoid either neglect or overwhelming through excessive stimulation, and to support their appropriate adaptive use.

It is well known that a mother needs to welcome, support, and appreciate her child's newly developing functions to help them flourish; that is, she has to invest them lovingly, including them in her relationship with her child. For some functions this maternal investment is especially crucial. However, even a mother's loving investment becomes unhelpful when it seeks to gratify her urges, rather than taking the form of calm modulated support.

When the mother is, for example, excited about, rather than glad and appreciative of, her child's beginning speech, she joins him at his level and the speech then tends to remain in the service of gratifying impulses instead of increasingly serving the whole personality. It becomes an end in itself rather than a tool. Several toddlers demonstrated very good early speech. Their speech was clear, there was an extensive vocabulary, and advanced use of syntax. It was capable of expressing not only needs but ideas, and of relating events in sequence and detail. Some of the mothers of these toddlers were so excited about this development that they repeatedly commented on it to everyone. They encouraged the child's talking, and wanted others to listen to him, regardless of whether the talking occurred at appropriate times, fit the situation, served communication, or encroached upon the rights of others. Some of the youngsters increasingly misused their talking to show off, to preoccupy the teacher, to invade others' speech or activities. At the same time, their use of speech for communication and thinking did not progress. They might talk a blue streak at circle time instead of listening, thinking, and responding verbally to the topic at hand. When asked about an activity they were working on, they started to relate at length what they had experienced at home instead of giving an answer or explanation. Sometimes such use of their speech was clearly geared to gratifying their aggressive or excited impulses, sometimes it served to ward off unpleasure; for example, when they changed the subject in order to avoid the hurt of not knowing something or not knowing how to do something. When the mothers were helped to realize their part in it and could support us in pointing out the difficulty to the child as well as in limiting the talking at these times, the children's speech began to serve them better and to progress.

Likewise, some mothers' inappropriate investment of their children's motor activity supported its continuing use for impulse gratification and did not help them to progress to curbing it for the sake of safety or to learn skills. They were so thrilled at the zest and speed of their toddler's tricycling, hammer bashing, or adventurous climbing that they did not notice, much less interfere, when the child repeatedly endangered himself and others. It was even hard for them to appreciate how scared he got when he rammed into a post or fell from a jungle gym, and they did not realize that he could not and would not learn the necessary skills with help because the frustrations of practicing got in the way of impulse gratification. Some mothers got quite cross with us for enforcing safety rules. Like their youngsters, they feared that limits and channeling of energy would spoil the fun of movement. Only when they could be helped to see that their children began to lag in real skills, and often got so afraid that they refused to climb or ride a tricycle, did they begin to work on this in themselves and with their child.

At the opposite extreme, it was striking to observe the toddler's need of mother's consistent investment of him in order to maintain any function. A mother's disinvestment markedly diminished the child's investment in and use of all his functions.

Karen would enter our room alone, stumbling along loose-limbed, disregarding her mother, who had stopped to hang up her coat in the hall closet and was chatting with another mother. Usually Karen also disregarded us, walked aimlessly from one activity to another, busied herself here or there, but never productively invested herself in a toy or materials. When we tried to help her, she could not use us or our words. Her eyes focused elsewhere, and when she noticed another child doing something else, she would suddenly leave and go off in that direction. But her interest was fleeting, even when she got as far as the other child, and often enough she changed course after a few steps to go after something else which had momentarily caught her attention. She had words but did not use them for communication. She could swing but would suddenly let go of her hold and fall. She could tricycle but did so without zest or purpose and would bump into things, forgetting herself, not hearing warnings. Although she looked around, she often did not appear to perceive.

Mother would stay near her and often tried to interest her in activities, but soon mother's attention would wander too, and quite often she actually absented herself (to use the bathroom, to get something from her coat, to adjust her hair) and, had we not intervened, she would not have prepared Karen for her absences. "Oh, it doesn't matter. I'll be right back. She'll be all right." And indeed Karen would pay little attention to mother's leaving and returning, and even to the preparation. Mother viewed Karen as "all right" and perhaps a casual onlooker would have agreed. After all, Karen was not upset, went along with what was expected without protest, kept apparently busy, knew how to talk and walk. In many ways mother regarded Karen's seeming lack of concern as an asset, sparing mother from guilt over separations at home, and allowing her to assume that Karen was comfortable everywhere with anyone.

Yet she was a caring mother and Karen was a well-cared for child. Mother was disturbed by her daughter's disinterest in learning and succeeding. What made the most helpful impact, however, was our pointing out that Karen acted as though mother did not matter and that we thought mother was really very important to Karen, just as Karen was for her. With the help of her treatment-via-the-parent, mother began to notice and pick up on Karen's subtle and often indirect responses to mother's physical and/or emotional unavailability. In Toddler Group mother and teachers made a concerted effort to help them stay in touch with one another. Karen soon responded by claiming mother in a close bodily way, with much lap sitting and holding, and later looking at books together during these times. They were recapturing an earlier close time from infancy. For a while Karen guarded their twosome so fiercely that she would not allow teachers or peers near them and refused to participate in teacher initiated activities, even with mother close by. With increased love came increased anger, first safely directed at others, then surfacing also toward mother. Most evident was the change in Karen's functions. Her motor control became zestful and purposeful. She became touchily protective of herself and her belongings. She started to communicate, and to share her astute perceptions and understanding of them. Interests emerged and were pursued, and even when she refused or discontinued an activity, she made a clear decision in lieu of the earlier bland disinvestment. Although Karen now showed strong upsets and was much harder to handle, she was also happier and mother was thrilled to have a "real" child.

With several other toddlers, the mother's disinvestment was only intermittent but still had an immediate and profound effect on the child. One little boy responded to his mother's periodic withdrawal by discontinuing everything he was doing—talking, playing, working, taking interest in and interacting with his surroundings—and simply sat on the floor pushing his little car aimlessly back and forth. One little girl would wander off, even out of the room and down the hall, "losing" herself and her self-investment as soon as her mother "lost" her when she became absorbed in something or someone else. The child would repeatedly get lost in stores while mother shopped. Some children reacted by becoming naughty. Although this served as a means of recapturing mother's attention, it also represented a loss of functions. Their running, tricycling, drawing, or cutting with scissors changed to heedless, aimless, or aggressive activity. Their speech became shrill, chattery, and intrusive without being directed to anyone in particular. They ignored what was happening around them, such as the arrival of a visitor, or suddenly reacted with fright to familiar people or events. The children were so sensitive to their mothers' temporary disinvestment that we often noticed the child's response before becoming aware of the mother's withdrawal, especially as it occurred while she remained physically in place. Only when we alerted her to her child's need of her, and often actually brought him back to her, did her sudden startle, as if returning from another world, reveal just how much she had been out of touch. There might be a glazed expression of incomprehension and an, "Oh, what were you doing? What was the trouble? I was just thinking about something (or I was just listening to so-and-so's mommy)."

THE NATURE OF THE CHILD'S INVESTMENT

The child's initial investment in a new function—in contrast to the mother's—needs to be fueled by his excited and aggressive urges. In time, and with mother's help, this energy is transformed and channeled for skilled adaptive uses. With Marjorie, described earlier (chapter 7), we had the opportunity to observe the effect of insufficient urge energy on her developing functions.

> At the time of her arrival in the foster home in a failure-to-thrive state, Marjorie did not walk or talk and showed minimal use of other functions. This appeared related to her prior inadequate mothering. With the help of the foster mother's relationship and support, Marjorie caught up and became an observant, competent, and skilled youngster. However, although she could exercise all functions, they lacked pleasure and zest and she showed no initiative. She spoke, walked, did activities, observed. She did everything whenever it was necessary or she was asked to, but never because she wanted to. The mother's support and appreciation of Marjorie's functions had helped them to develop maturationally but had not made up for the child's own lack of investment with urge energy.
>
> This changed only when, no doubt with the help of the mother–child relationship, Marjorie's urges were stimulated and started to infuse her functions. At first this manifested itself in less self-control and increased use of functions for impulse gratification; for example, she chattered excitedly out of turn and danced and jumped around when she was supposed to sit still. There was less conformity but much more pleasure, zest,

and initiative. She regained control with time, without losing her verve.

We observed a similar lag in urge investment where there had been no inadequacy or discontinuity in the mother–child relationship, but in cases where the child had suffered major prolonged illness and medical–surgical treatments during infancy.

We observed a very different interference with very overstimulated youngsters. They invested their developing functions with an excess of urge energy which caused them conflict and made it harder for them to bring the functions under their control. In these cases it appeared that the excessively stimulated urges were beyond the personality's capacity for channeling them into more adaptive use.

FUNCTIONS DEVELOPING INDEPENDENTLY OF THE MOTHER'S SUPPORT

Although we take it for granted that the mother–child relationship and specific maternal attitudes affect the development of all functions, the extent to which they play a part varies.

We were impressed to find that the toddler's *memory* appears to develop rather independently, is invariably excellent, and serves them very well. Mothers rarely actively support this personality tool. In fact, they tend to disregard it and to be amazed that the child remembers and what he remembers. Perhaps this is in part due to the fact that memory does develop without the mother's help and is not affected by what she wants him to remember. Confronted with evidence of her toddler's remembering, either in words or in action, many a mother realized with something of a shock just how much he is a person in his own right. Sometimes she was startled by how far back into the past her child's memory reached, sometimes by his remembering details of a shared experience that differed greatly from her own memory of it.

It was not surprising to us or even to the mothers, for that matter, that the child often remembered events associated with needs and impulse gratification, such as urinating in the bushes at the zoo or tweaking the nose of the woman who was too intrusive (see chapter 3). More surprising was the fact that many memories of a less personal nature were very meaningful. One toddler, for example, remembered seeing a star in the evening sky. Her mother disputed this at first, but then confirmed it when the child reminded her of the specific circumstances. Such incidents were frequent, with some children remembering at age 2 events that had taken place before they were 1 year old. These were sometimes events that had not been talked about later nor were they part of a family experience or of family remembering, as may be the case with special occasions. Some of these memories were expressed in actions, and it took mother some time before she understood what it was about. On being told that a baby-sitter of long ago would visit them, one toddler put up her arms, recalling that sitter's special way of helping with dressing.

Strikingly too, the children (like the little girl who saw the star) were always very sure of their memories and stood up for their veracity, not only when mother could not remember and confirm the content, but also when she definitely contradicted her child. This independent ownership of the memory function was not only evident in well-functioning toddlers. We observed it also in the most disturbed children who showed much interference or lag with some of their other personality tools. The mother nevertheless helps her child by respecting and valuing his ability to remember. This assists him in appreciating it and feeling appreciated for it, and enables him to use it pleasurably, enhancing his self-esteem. As one toddler said proudly, "I am a good rememberer."

Sensory *perception* is another function which appears to develop autonomously, and like memory (which of course draws on what has been perceived), often focuses on a world that is different from that of the mother. We had appreciated the toddlers' astute visual perception before Toddler Group started, and had therefore geared our educational approach to supporting it by alerting the parents to its existence, and also emphasizing the need to conform and discuss all the potentially puzzling sights the children might notice (chapter 2). This expectation was borne out. There was never a minor change or difference in the room or in the people which went unnoticed by the children, although it often escaped the attention of the mothers, be it a tiny Band-Aid on a teacher's finger, a differently arranged shelf, or a peer's speech difficulty. To an extent, the youngsters' seeing focused on "loaded" matters (toileting, aggression), but at least equally, if not more so, on differences which related to or threatened their vulnerable integrity, as discussed earlier (chapter 5). This included bodily differences, suggestive of injury or anomaly, and differences in routines or setting (visitors, new equipment, rearrangement of furniture), viewed as a potential upset of the familiar safety. In addition, the children focused intensely on everything at or below their own height. They noticed the least little crumb on the floor, the tiniest bug on the ground outdoors, and they found the most hidden piece of a toy, wherever it might have rolled out of sight of the adults. But they were oblivious to what could be seen above. Learning to see the sun and clouds required a great deal of adult help. Even helicopters and tall construction rigs near our playground needed much pointing out and assistance in guiding their vision, although the noise scared or fascinated them and they wanted to know just where it came from. The same youngsters who quickly pointed out an ant on the ground, never looked up at the trees. They were amazed when we pointed out the rich crop of mulberries on the branches just above them, although they had spotted them on the ground right away.

Toddlers' hearing is also extremely acute, more so than that of adults, and particularly sensitive to loudness, which is always disturbing, unless they produce it themselves. Many children who did not seem to endow noise with aggressive meaning and were not afraid of specific noisy things, did not like loud noises. We took care all along to keep our songs as well as room and activities at moderate levels of loudness because the children reacted to a higher level at once, sometimes clearly stating their dislike, sometimes responding by seemingly trying to drown it out by making louder sounds themselves. When one child used the differently pitched drumming cans; we made a point of warning the others ahead, or of helping them to tolerate it because it was a "safe" noise. At times when the nearby hospital helicopter, construction machines, or ambulance sirens made a big and to them disturbing noise, we helped by showing and explaining what it was and how it worked. At first we did not appreciate that the ordinary street traffic noise upset them as much as what we considered unusual noise. We later made it a practice during the first months of the school year to put small ladders up against the playground fence so that the toddlers could watch the cars and trucks, and familiarize themselves with and understand the source of the noise. At times, however, the noises they noticed and questioned were so faint that we had to strain to hear them and help with locating and explaining them; for example, the flushing noise of an upstairs toilet, the barely audible hum of the fluorescent light. As with vision, hearing too seemed prompted by concerns over safety and interests related to anger and excitement.

It seems that the young child's hypersensitive vision and hearing are related to his difficulty in making sense of the reality to which his perceptions alert him. When a child could see as well as hear the truck, and integrate this with our explanation, he was better able to screen out the previously vivid perceptions. After they knew what the street noises were about, most children paid no attention to them. Similarly, even adults hear all the minor noises in a new house but disregard them later, when they have understood what makes these noises and why. Children are notorious for overhearing everything they don't understand or are not supposed to understand. In part this is motivated by their impulses, but in part it stems from the puzzlement and potential danger of the ununderstandable.

By contrast, the toddlers readily screen out or ignore adults' words which are all too familiar, such as requests and admonitions. Somewhat different is some children's tuning out of all words, not even responding to being repeatedly called by name. With some toddlers this was so marked that the mothers were concerned about hearing loss. Sometimes we could point out that the child heard faint distant noises. Some had hearing tests which proved their hearing was normal. This kind of not hearing invariably related to not being listened to by mother, usually because she tuned out the child. Mothers tended to be unaware of their disinvestment, but it was readily observed by others. In cases like that of Karen, described above, where disinvestment was quite pervasive, the child's not listening was not so selective but affected all or most of their hearing.

For some time we were quite puzzled by the toddlers' seeming inattentiveness to smells. Many mothers spontaneously pointed out good smells emanating from the kitchen, or the strong smell of some flowers, and as teachers we made a concerted effort to offer and draw their attention to different smells. The children did not seem to notice them on their own, and often were not interested in the smells the adults noticed. They did not even comment on bad smells, such as from rotting plants. The following incident finally helped us to appreciate the toddler's very different world of smells, and their acute perception of them.

> Tom had never shown interest in smells throughout his year in our Group. His mother had periodically drawn his attention to special smells, but this did not further his interest, although he politely sniffed and acknowledged it. A year later I met him in the hall and greeted him happily. "Oh, you so smell of Toddler Group," he replied. When I asked him whether it was a good smell, he affirmed this enthusiastically and added that the good Toddler Group smell always reminds him of Toddler Group. I was surprised, not least because I had not realized that Toddler Group had a special smell, much less that I smelled like it.

We all know, of course, how often toddlers smell rather than just stroke or feel their blankie or stuffed toy. For toddlers in day care the most meaningful concrete reminder of mother during a long day is something of hers that smells of her, a shirt, nightie, scarf. These are the things the children choose to keep whenever they are allowed to make a choice. These were also the things the very young chose to keep and nuzzle after the loss of their mother through death. In day care or bereavement, some youngsters would, at times of longing, reach for mother's hat, sweater, or robe, bury their face in it, and inhale deeply. Nonsmelling items, such as keys, wallet, or even her purse, were much less satisfactory, and photos meant very little, since the child's image of mother rarely corresponded with that of the photo (E. Furman, 1974, 1984).

Tom's "good Toddler Group smell" helped us to appreciate that it is not only mother who is so prominently perceived in terms of smell but all people and places. Much older children sometimes comment, "It still smells the same," when they return to a house or place they used to know when very young. Nursery schoolers often comment on smells. When taken to a farm, for example, smells are usually their first and main impression, but by that age smells evoke a mixture of disgust and fascination. For the toddler, the world of smells is not conflicted. It is very much his own and very serviceable. Mothers know that the blankie must not be washed lest it lose its smell, they often use the phrases "smelling clean" and "smelling yukky" around the child's toileting, and smile indulgently at the occasional affectionate "Mommy, you smell so good." They do not share their child's intense and ever present smell perceptions, however, and do not use smells to orient themselves in the world the way the child does. And he, in turn, is only mildly interested in their selected smells, which they judge good or bad so differently from him, and which almost always exclude familiar people and places. Perhaps in our society the mother's role with smell is predominantly inhibiting and redirecting, rather than facilitating.

FUNCTIONS CLOSELY DEPENDENT ON MATERNAL SUPPORT

When the mother's role in helping her toddler achieve bodily self-care was discussed, the successive steps in this process were linked to the necessary change in the nature of her relationship with him. To a considerable extent, the steps of doing for, doing with, standing by to admire, and independent functioning, apply as much to the mother–child interactions around functions as they do with bodily self-care. So does the concomitant need for mother to change her relationship, that is, to relate with her child more as a separate person. But there are also marked differences, not only between bodily care and functions, but between functions.

Given adequate physical and mental endowment on the child's part and consistent and good-enough investment of him on the mother's part, some personality tools develop without mother's direct assistance, and her role becomes significant only at certain stages in the developmental process. This, as discussed above, applies to memory, perception, and in some ways to motor control. These functions require from the start mother's recognition of her toddler as a separate person. She can support their development only insofar as she has adapted her relationship accordingly. When she lags, there are often head-on struggles between her and the child. There are many times, for example, when a mother wants to carry her toddler, but he screams and kicks to be put down, insisting on doing his own walking. Her excuse, "It takes too long to wait for him," is valid, but if the confrontation happens repeatedly it implies that she considers it still her function to move him around and cannot allow him to own his ability to walk.

Some other functions depend much more closely on mother's facilitation. She is closely involved in their every progressive step and prepares herself for it. She has time to adapt her investment. *Speech* is known to depend very much on mother–child interaction from infancy on. Our observations indicate, however, that, even when the preparatory steps have proceeded successfully, the child's effective use of speech develops best when the mother has, to a sufficient extent, begun to relate to her child as a separate loved person. She then regards his speech as his own and listens to him to learn about *his* ideas, without assuming that she already knows what he is thinking, feeling, or going to say. Nonverbal communication, however effective, and mutual cooing and babbling, however enjoyable for both, do not entail this; nor does the mother's mere listening to him, which may represent a self-gratification for her, rather than a means of understanding another person's communication. We had several children whose speech development lagged, and several others whose good early speech skills failed to progress and/or were not used for communication, until their mothers could be helped to invest and support the child's speech as his own function, to listen to it as a way of finding out about his own inner life.

No function, however, seems as dependent on the mother's step-by-step participation as *understanding reality*. Although the young child's perceptions are so acute and develop so early and independently, he is at a loss to interpret them without mother's help. He does not trust his own assessment, even with the simplest things, until she has confirmed it.

> One day at snack there was a lively conversation about butterflies. Mindy, 22-months-old, spoke up proudly, "I have butterflies on my curtains." Then she suddenly looked bewildered, turned to her mother and asked, "Are there butterflies on my curtains?" "Yes," replied mother. Mindy then repeated her proud announcement as though her previous one had not counted: "There are butterflies on my curtains."

This does not imply that the child unquestioningly accepts mother's view of reality, or that his function is not affected if he accepts it unquestioningly despite inner doubt. This is particularly evident in instances where mother's feelings are at odds with her own and the toddler's perception of facts. Children quickly sense which topics and events mother does not want to notice and explain and they comply by not asking about them. Often they give the impression of not even perceiving or thinking about them. In other words, they perceive and adapt to her feelings about a particular subject. For example, in the Toddler Group we made a concerted effort to confirm and discuss the youngsters' potentially unwelcome perceptions and helped the children and mothers to explain and understand them in realistic terms. Among these topics was the beginning and end of life, which came up repeatedly in connection with plants and gardening. Although the mothers participated enthusiastically in this part of the curriculum, supported our attitudes, and recognized the children's observations, their difficulties sometimes led them to confuse the child about the reality.

> When our sweet potato had grown well in a glass jar for several months, sprouting lots of roots and trailing vines, it started to

rot and die. The children followed this closely, and we prepared them for digging the remains into our vegetable garden where they would further deteriorate and become part of the earth and enrich it. When the little boy had completed this burying job with our help, his mother said, "See, now it's lying there all cozy, sleeping." Her son looked bewildered but said nothing. I intervened, pointing out that mommy, he, and I knew it was really dead. Mother caught herself and confirmed what I had said. He was relieved and told his peers, "I dug it in. It's dead" [E. Furman, 1990].

When we had carrots for snack, we usually cut off the tops, put them in a shallow dish of water, and watched the green sprouts grow. One day a child was a bit rough in handling them and his mother warned: "If you touch them again, you'll have carrots growing all over out of your head." Her son looked utterly bewildered, reached out to touch the carrots again with one hand, and rubbed his other hand through his hair, evidently feeling around for the predicted growing carrots. But he did not question mother's dictum. I sympathized with his bewilderment and suggested mother help him. She took back her warning, saying she had just joked. This proved even more bewildering to him. I then added that mommy had really wanted him to be gentle with the carrot tops because they can get hurt easily and then would not grow well.

When the mothers could support the children's learning about the life cycle of plants, the toddlers readily extended it themselves to their past and current experiences with animals and people. They told of their goldfish who had died, the squirrel that had been run over, the bird found dead in a snow pile. They compared the deaths, their causes, and forms of disposal of the corpses. They and their mothers also used this base of understanding to discuss the deaths of people they heard about, as well as of the grandparent or old neighbor they had known well. But when the mother could not acknowledge these more painful deaths, the child did not assess the new reality in terms of his earlier understanding.

Janie and her mother made several trips out of town to visit her seriously ill grandmother. They went there again when she had died, at which time mother attended the funeral while relatives stayed with Janie. Mother only told Janie she would not see grandmother ever again. Janie did not question her and did not talk about grandmother in Toddler Group. With mother's permission we told Janie and her mom how sorry we were that her Grandma had died, but she changed the subject. Death had not been mentioned by mother or child.

Within a few weeks Janie began to talk a great deal of her worry about airplanes. Later she got more worried when the family planned a vacation where they would travel by plane, and when her father and older sister were to fly somewhere on their own, she was even more upset. It turned out that Janie thought each time someone goes by plane it might lead to never seeing him or her again. Although she knew about death with plants and insects, knew about grandmother's illness, and had witnessed the family upset at the time of the funeral, she had taken over mother's distorted reality about grandmother's death and disregarded her own knowledge and observations.

Yet often toddlers defend the veracity of their perceptions and realistic assessment of them in the face of mother's denial or distortion. When mother explained Barbara's defiant behavior as due to fatigue, the child retorted, "I'm not tired. I am angry."

One day in the hallway, Max correctly informed his mother, "There is a poo smell. Come over here and smell it. It's from her" (pointing to an adult). Mother said she did not smell anything and tried to change the subject. Max insisted once more, then seemingly gave up and walked toward the door where I was waiting for them. He greeted me with "There was a poo smell from that lady."

Like the boy in Andersen's fairy tale "The Emperor's New Clothes," young children often can and do use their perceptions to assess reality very accurately, especially when the adults wish they would not. Young children, and our toddlers too, assess reality in terms of the bodily needs, impulses, and feelings which make up their world. Insofar as he had been helped to own and know his bodily self and make sense of its sensations

and rhythms, the young child perceives and assesses these behaviors in himself and others with stunning and often embar-
rassing accuracy. Insofar as he has been able to count on
mother's truthful confirmation and acceptance of his perceptions and assessments in these areas, he has come to own and
trust them, and will even stand up for them against her on the
few occasions when she lets him down. His persistence at these
times indicates that he trusts himself and her enough to feel he
can convince her, bring her around, and often he is right. Just
as the child who keeps on protesting mother's bodily care of him
signals his justified hope that she will recognize and support
his readiness for self-care, so the child who stands up for his
perceived reality shows that he feels he can count on her confirmation. By contrast, the child who has not been helped to
know and own his body, needs, impulses, and feelings is at a
real loss to assess this inner reality in himself and in others, or
cannot trust his assessment. He is simply bewildered, as was the
case with the child whose mother declared the sweet potato was
cozily sleeping, and with the one whose mother warned him of
carrots growing on his head. In the former instance, the child
would have been helped most if the mother had been able to
acknowledge her personal discomfort with death; in the latter
instance, the most appropriate help would have been for the
mother to acknowledge her anger and apologize for her threat.
Both children had, no doubt, sensed their mothers' feelings,
and it was this which needed to be confirmed to help them
make sense of their perceptions and to understand the external
reality of the potato and carrots. We do not know Janie's initial
response to her mother's distortion of the reality regarding
grandmother's death. Judging, however, by Janie's overall difficulty in knowing her body, needs, and feelings and mother's
corresponding difficulty in helping her in these areas, it is likely
that Janie readily acquiesced in mother's interpretation of reality. In the same way, she let mother decide what was good to
eat, when diapers should be changed, and whether Janie was
angry or scared.

When the toddlers are beginning to gain trust in their
ability to understand their needs, impulses, and feelings, they
also show and tell us how they use it to assess the inanimate

outside reality. In that sphere it does not serve them so well. We learn that the steamshovel eats a whole lot of leaves, that the motorcycles are very angry, that the car makes a poo-poo smell. One child was incredulous on being told that the carrots put into the top of the food grinder would come out mashed from its lower front opening because, "What you eat always comes out your backside." The steps toward distinguishing animate from inanimate and bodily–emotional from neutral, take a long time, and proceed along with the maturation of other faculties, such as logical thinking. And again, they depend closely on the mother's help. This help includes empathy with and respect for the child's view of the reality so as to enable him to contrast as well as harmonize the differing assessments as well as to preserve and support his valuing of his functions. To regard the steamshovel as a hefty eater is not stupid or laughable, it is understandable, though incorrect. The young child's frame of reference is never fully supplanted. When, as adults, we face a very unfamiliar reality we still draw on this early base to interpret it. The new computer may be jocularly seen as eating and spitting out, a concept not dissimilar from the 2-year-old's steamshovel.

THE EARLY CONSCIENCE

A conscience is not a personality tool, like speech or memory, but it resembles one, in the sense that it develops step by step during the early years, becomes an integral part of us, and serves us, guiding our behavior. As adults, if all has gone well enough, we count on our conscience to embody our values and standards, to make us feel good when we have done our best to live up to them, warn us when we are tempted to do otherwise, plague us with guilt when we have gone astray, and prompt us to make amends and try harder the next time.

The earliest conscience is no such reasonable and reliable inner helper. Like the toddler himself, his conscience has a limited view of the world, what it wants it wants omnipotently, immediately, and perfectly, and when thwarted it brooks no compromise and punishes its owner with an angry vengeance.

The children's guilt and self-diminishment were intense, stemming from inner prohibitions which were harsh and from standards and ideals which far exceeded their ability to perform accordingly. We constantly had to help them to tone down their self-criticism, to forgive themselves for mistakes, to make up for wrongdoings so that they could repair their self-esteem, weigh their positives against the negatives, and have some trust in being able to do better in time. The mothers were always surprised by their toddlers' expectations for themselves and by the extent of their despair when they did not live up to them. It stood in stark contrast to the mothers' view of the children's misbehaviors, namely, that they were a sign of not knowing right from wrong and needing to have the rules spelled out. With toileting, for example, a child's setback was readily seen as his not wanting or not trying hard enough to be clean. It was at first difficult for the mothers to recognize and empathize with how bad he felt about himself and hopeless about ever making it, needing her assuring and trusting support. The mothers of these children were not unduly harsh or de-manding, but they misunderstood the child's inner world. They also got angry themselves and this lent a forceful and punitive edge to their spelling out of the rules. They did not realize that they were actually reinforcing the already harsh early chunks of conscience inside the child's mind. They would have been shocked to think that, from infancy on, their "no's," their disap-proving faces and manner, their reprimanding phrases, not to mention angry yells, had, as it were, been swallowed whole, and with a big dash of punitiveness which was much more threatening than the parents' intent. Of course, the parents' kindness and loving are absorbed as well, but these will only in time soften and tame those unrelenting early chunks of con-science and mold them into an inner monitor with reasonable expectations. In the meantime, however, the young child's guilt feelings are so painful and hard to bear that his immature mind uses every available means to avoid them. Holly (chapter 3) attacked and yelled at *me* when she felt bad about having used a puzzle without first getting my permission. Bess (chapter 3), after a hard day, turned on her mother with, "You are a bad mommy," and had to be reminded that she might really be angry at herself. Different children found different ways of dealing with their inner discomfort:

> Ellen sat next to me at snack. Swinging her legs vigorously all the time, she kicked me several times. At first I moved a little to the side, then I pointed it out, and suggested she be the boss of her legs so they would stay in her space. In response to this Ellen's face clouded over angrily and she scolded me: "You should say you're sorry." We discussed the mix-up, and when she was able to own her guilt, she apologized.
>
> On another occasion Ellen had made a scribble on another child's paper and had some difficulty owning up. She had been angry when confronted and did not follow mother's suggestion to apologize to the child. Ellen did something else. She took the teachers' stack of paper from the shelf, laid out a sheet on the table for each person, put crayons with them, and announced that they could now all make their own nice picture. We acknowledged her wish to put things right, but pointed out also that she had taken the teachers' paper and was acting a bit like a bossy teacher who told everyone what to do. Perhaps she felt it would be better to be the teacher than to be Ellen. Ellen thought about this a bit, collected the papers, put them back, and made an apology picture for the child on whose paper she had scribbled.

> When Damon once knocked down a sand castle I had made for another child, he started to attack me and yell at me. I wondered whether he knew he felt bad and perhaps expected me to punish him. I told him it had made me angry but I would not punish him. What could he do to feel better about it? Damon stopped, and after a moment's thought made a sincere verbal apology which I accepted. Then he resumed his attacking. I wondered whether he still felt bad, and if so, why. He then muttered the child's name whose sand castle I had been working on, but who was playing elsewhere and had not seen what he had done. Did he think he ought to apologize to that child too? He nodded and, with a bit of help, sought out the child and apologized.

> Adam was sometimes very angry at his mother at home and got even more angry when she reprimanded him. For weeks, though, he greeted us in Toddler Group with a long account of all his bad behaviors. Not only had this not been discussed with

or prompted by his mother, it usually surprised and even embarrassed her. In part, Adam perhaps looked to the teachers for reassurance or punishment, but he usually felt so miserable about himself that his confessions simply implied, "This is what has been uppermost in my mind." In the middle of a game or snack he would similarly suddenly blurt out something mean he had perpetrated long ago.

When the toddler's early conscience far exceeds his capacity to use it helpfully as an inner guide, the guilt becomes unbearable and tends to be warded off in maladaptive ways, such as turning the tables and blaming others or feeling bad at the wrong time. Parents and caregivers help best by recognizing this with the child and supporting adaptive means of coping. Bess, for example, was not helped by mother's acceptance of the blame ("You are a bad Mommy"). She needed to own her anger at herself, to view it as exaggerated in the opinion of the adults, and be assured of her ability and their help to achieve better behavioral control in the future. Adam, who always confessed his wrongdoings later, did not need to be reprimanded more forcefully at the time of misbehaving, but did need help in knowing that he will not like himself for it and would feel better if he could exercise more self-control or, at least, make up right away for what he had just done. Such support helps the child to know and own his conscience, and maintains or reestablishes empathic mother–child communication.

CHAPTER 10

Playing, Learning, and Socializing

When parents are asked what they would like to say to their toddlers about enrolling in a group, they usually reply, "It'll be a nice place with lots of toys and friends to play with and lots of new things to do." Yet playing, interacting with peers, and learning are complex developmental achievements. They require a degree of personality maturity where just about all aspects of functioning have sufficiently developed and become integrated. The child needs to be relatively free of the pressure of bodily needs and assured of them being met when they arise (either because mother is with him or because he can care for himself); his impulses need to be in good enough control. He needs to be interested in activities, derive pleasure from the process of pursuing them, and gratification in achievement. This is far from where the personality stands at the beginning of the toddler phase. One hopes it may develop toward such a level, little by little, with the help of parents and educators, by the end of the phase. In thinking about a toddler group, parents do not realize this, and especially, they never include their own role, much less that of the teacher, as though playing, learning, and peer relationships could come about without this facilitating bridge and were stimulated by the mere availability of toys, materials, and other children.

In many mother–toddler groups, mother arrives with her child, takes off and stores his clothes, tells him to "go play" and then sits back. Sometimes she chats with other mothers, sews, or reads a magazine, sometimes she anxiously watches her toddler across the room, torn as to whether to go to him or stay put. If she does go over to "get him started," to extricate him from a tussle over a toy, to rescue him from an exchange of blows or from making a mess at the sand table, she limits her intervention to the minimum, and returns to her seat as quickly as possible. And if he is hesitant to "go play," returns "too often," or wants to stay by her "too long," she feels a bit uneasy, encourages him to leave her, and entices him by pointing out all the supposedly attractive toys. Similarly, when introducing their toddler to a program where he will eventually stay without them, mothers tend to hope that he won't need them, will use the toys and join peers in play, all without first building a relationship with the caregiver and effecting a comfortable transition from mother to mother substitute. The mothers' unawareness of their importance to the child and to his functioning is further borne out by their assumption that their child's liking of or interest in an activity they have pursued together at home will continue to provide pleasure in their absence. Mothers believe that the attraction of new toys or materials will of itself lead their toddler to want to learn about them and use them constructively, and that his fascination with other children and their behavior and activities will automatically translate into engaging with them in enjoyable mutual interactions.

At intake, regardless of the nature of the group program, mothers tell how their child loves stories, loves to make sandpies, loves to watch the youngsters in the street or playground. They are then dismayed to see or hear about their child not even wanting to sit down for stories, not attending to them, and sucking his thumb, or bothering others instead. They are equally dismayed that he lies in the sandbox or throws the sand around instead of making nice pies, and that he attacks, fears, or avoids the other children, instead of viewing them as friends. These mothers had simply disregarded the crucial significance of their invested presence and participation. They did not appreciate, for example, that it is not the books that are loved, but mother reading them with the child on her lap. When the professional staff understands the child's needs and plans for the mothers' active participation or help with gradual separation, the hardest job is to persuade the mothers of their importance for the child's motivation for and mastery of the new tasks (E. Furman, 1984). When the staff shares the mothers' disregard of themselves, either in the sense of also disregarding the caregivers' role or of assuming that they are more important than the mother and can proceed without her, the child often never progresses to real playing, learning, and peer relations. In these instances, the mothers and caregivers tend to misjudge the child's behavior. They see him going from toy to toy or tagging along with an older child and erroneously view this as "playing well" with toys and other children. He may repetitively push a little toy or car back and forth, and that will be mistaken for loving to play with cars. Wanting to have and do whatever another child is about, and dashing over to intrude is described as eagerness to play with others. Getting all excited over a new toy or activity but soon losing interest is seen as needing the challenge of new activities to avoid boredom. Sooner or later, however, and sometimes only after months or years, the child's failure to progress becomes a serious interference in his ability to meet phase-appropriate expectations and his difficulties have to be recognized. This tends to lead to tension between parents and caregivers over who is to blame, and more often than not, the child himself is blamed. But the true initial cause, namely, having disregarded the role of the mother at the time of entry into the group, is rarely traced.

We were very familiar with all these issues from our observations of and work with older children entering nursery school, as well as from observing in and consulting for toddler groups and their staff in the community. We planned our Toddler Group with this in mind, and during the intake procedure as well as at the open house, share with the parents not only the points outlined above, but also why the mothers need to participate in all of the child's activities during classes. We discuss with the mothers the point that building the relationship with the teacher is a major developmental task, and that work toward it proceeds via the mother–child relationship (chapter 2). We and the mothers had nevertheless underestimated the mother's role at each step. The present discussion of play, learning, and socializing will therefore highlight this aspect.

PLAY

In our Toddler Group, all the youngsters took some time before they were able to play in the true sense, namely by endowing symbolic objects with personal meaning and using them to create an experience of their own making in "pretend" form (E. Furman, 1985a). For some this achievement came spontaneously at a point when they had mastered the adjustment to the new environment of the Toddler Group and gained, or regained, a measure of inner peace in relation to themselves and to their mothers. With others, play developed only with the help of adult pleasurable initiative and participation. Still others could never play, not even during their later preschool and kindergarten years.

This does not mean that the children did not handle dolls, push doll strollers, explore the dishes and utensils in the kitchen corner, line up the toy animals, and push little cars or trainsets. They did all these things, but insofar as they persisted for any length of time, they used them in the manner of the multiskill toys, the puzzles, pegboards, shape or color matching games, bead stringing, and similar activity sets. That is to say, they used them to investigate, to understand what they were, and how they worked, and to master them in the sense of accomplishing the implied task, such as hooking up all the train carriages, making the cars go, or filling all the holes on the pegboard. Many of them would also play by joining or imitating another's play; for example, by serving or being served a pretend meal alongside a peer who had initiated the play, or driving a car on a block-built road as they had seen another child do. However, they could not come up with ideas of their own or elaborate and vary the other's play by adding individual themes. In some instances we saw what initially looked like play, such as stacking cars, sorting adult and baby animals, or putting out the dishes; but, like a stuck phonograph record, the activity remained repetitive, and often joyless and incapable of progression or resolution. In some instances, the beginning of play was quickly overtaken by impulses—the doll plates jumbled into a pile, the cars bashing into things, the animals strewn around. It was tempting to regard these behaviors as prestages of play, early forms which would develop into play, but this expectation was not borne out.

TRANSITIONAL OBJECTS—THE FIRST TOY

Many years ago, D. W. Winnicott (1953), a pediatrician and psychoanalyst, pointed out the significance and importance of the older infant's first toy—his blankie, piece of satin binding, or earliest soft toy. Winnicott related the child's "creation" of this meaningful possession to the newly gained awareness of a separateness between mother and self, a space the infant attempts to fill and bridge with the help of this object. For this reason Winnicott called it a "transitional object," representing mother, child, and the transitional space between them. Creating this transitional object is not only a big developmental step in itself, but underlies the child's later ability to play and, later yet, to appreciate and enjoy art which similarly conveys meanings in symbolic form. We therefore paid close attention to whether or not the toddlers had transitional objects, how they were using them, and to what extent this affected their ability to play. And we found that this development depends as much on the child's as on the mother's growth in their relationship.

Some toddlers brought their transitional objects and, as expected, used them in their play. But many others did not. Some toddlers used a blankie or a special soft toy. They relied on it for comfort as well as for aggressive discharge (biting, crumpling, throwing down) or for gratification of excitement (to tickle, to hold in their crotch), but they did not use it to play; they did not feed it, make it take a trip, or go on a visit. Some did not have a transitional object but could or could be helped to play.

With many, however, the history and nature of a transitional object was difficult to determine. With several children, for example, it seemed that they had adopted the bottle as their transitional object. The bottle was then either taken away or its use was restricted to home or to bedtime. In these instances the mothers treated the bottle as an infantile form of feeding, but it never occurred to them that it served their children in a different way. Yet it was also true that no toddler attempted to use his bottle for symbolic play. There were other cases where an early and special soft toy had been lost or destroyed. Again the mothers had not thought of this object as something especially valuable for the child, and did not consider its disappearance of importance. Sometimes they had offered another toy which, even if accepted, did not really replace the first one and remained something the mother, rather than the child, had chosen. There were also several instances where the mother had interfered by insisting that there had to be several blankies so mother could wash any one when she considered it dirty. Some children accepted this and used the alternating blankies, but they were not their very own. And some mothers had so little "feel" for the idea of a transitional object that they took over altogether and simply picked out a "toy of the day" to give to their child to hold. There were also mothers who accepted the child's use of his blankie or teddy as a comforting device but not as a potential symbol, and some regarded the transitional object with almost hostile suspicion, fearing that the child would never give it up. The mothers tolerated it reluctantly, conveyed their disapproval, and deliberately or surreptitiously discouraged its use. For example, these mothers were glad when the transitional object had been left in the car, and fetched it only when the child totally despaired without it.

These variations helped us to appreciate how much the opportunity to choose, invest, and keep a transitional object depended on the mother's attitude to it; that is to say, to what extent the mother could relate to her child as a separate loved person whose functioning she respected and valued, felt with and supported, yet who was also still sufficiently a part of herself so that she could care for his transitional object as if it were her own. Above all, within this subtle balance of investments, could she share in the symbolic value of the transitional object and use it as a means of mutual communication? Insofar as the mothers succeeded in this, the transitional object became the springboard for more elaborate symbolic play; but without the mother's active support the transitional object could not serve in this way.

Around 7 months of age, during the time she was weaning herself from nursing, Lisa took to her stuffed monkey in a special way. According to her mother, she singled "him" out to hold and sleep with, leaving other soft toys at the end of her crib. She threw him out repeatedly to be retrieved when in her playpen. She wanted him along on walks and rides, nuzzled and bit him, and pushed him at mother or gave him to her to hold. Mother joined in, sometimes talking to or for monkey, sometimes hugging him as he was handed over or thrown down. She appreciated his good smell and never washed him. She carefully mended his loose arm and bare spots when Lisa showed concern over the results of her wear and tear of him. Mother always made sure he was not forgotten or left behind whenever Lisa had brought him along and, when he had been deliberately left at home, she rejoiced with Lisa on reuniting with him on their return.

By the time Lisa was 10 months old, she gave monkey pretend food and drinks and around 1 year of age, mother helped Lisa dress him, give him pretend baths, and push him in the stroller. By 18 months, monkey was still Lisa's favorite but she had considerably enlarged her "family" with the addition of other toys, and initiated quite elaborate play sequences with them. During the day, she always involved mother in them sooner or later; when in her bed at nap and night time, she played on her own. Often though, Lisa shared the contents of these playtimes when mother came to get her up and when the positions of the toys (in, out, or at the far corner of the bed) or their changed attire (wrapped in blanket, teething ring around their neck, jacket taken off) were noted by mother or pointed out by Lisa. In this way, mother and child continued to share this symbolic world and to enjoy their communication in it. By this time, mother had long since also added some of her own symbols to the play. She had sewn clothes for monkey, bought a doll tea set and introduced its use, pretended that she wanted

more or different items served, and allowed Lisa to accept, reject, or vary these new ideas.

Cindy had used a blankie since the latter part of her first year.
A year later, in Toddler Group, she was continuing to use it in
a seemingly similar fashion, for comfort and to mistreat. Her
mother tolerated it reluctantly. She had initially not wanted
Cindy to bring it to Toddler Group, hoping to discourage its
use, and sharing her worry that Cindy might never give it up.
When it became evident that Cindy was at a loss without it at
times, as well as after discussion with the therapist and teachers,
mother relented and appreciated that Cindy used it to contain
herself at times of minor stress. But Cindy did not play at all.
Asked about this, mother at first claimed that Cindy played a
great deal at home with her two older siblings.

Continued lack of play in Toddler Group prompted further
exploration. It turned out that the siblings used Cindy in their
play (e.g., to be their baby in pretend family play) but she never
initiated the play and did not contribute ideas. She was their
living toy. Mother herself did not play with Cindy. They never
communicated in symbolic form. We began to initiate play with
Cindy and mother, taking our clues from Cindy's activities. Since
she zestfully pushed the empty doll stroller, we asked if she
would want to give the doll baby a ride, helped her to put the
seatbelt around it, later wondered if it might be cold, and helped
to wrap it in a blanket, accompanied her on her "walk," and
talked about what a nice mommy she was and how her baby
liked it. Cindy was happily intrigued and asked for the game
repeatedly. With mother joining in, we "graduated" to a pretend
meal. Cindy now not only became active in serving and naming
the foods she was preparing, but brought over her blankie to
put on mother's lap and in this way had it participate. Soon
she brought a previously unused stuffed dog from home. She
introduced it to us and served it food too. Then the dog did a
dance. For some time Cindy needed our participation and
mother's as she began to branch out to use additional symbols—the toy animals, the blocks to make eating troughs and
houses for them. Mother could not play enough herself to enter
in with additional ideas or variations the way the teachers did,
but she could share and appreciate Cindy's pleasure and tune
into ideas that stemmed from shared experiences at home. She
also intervened in the siblings' misuse of Cindy, insisted that

Cindy be respected as an equal partner in their games, and protected Cindy's own play from untoward intrusions. During the next several months, playing became one of Cindy's own ways of dealing creatively with inner and outer experiences.

In the course of being helped to play, Cindy herself made the link to her transitional object, her blankie, by bringing it to join our pretend meal on mother's lap. Perhaps she could do that because mother had somewhat changed her attitude to the blankie. The crucial ingredient, however, was the teachers' playing and enlisting mother's participation in the play. Several other children began to play with this help without linking it to their transitional object. Indeed, a number of children who had never had a transitional object played well or "learned" to play.

PLAYING AS COMMUNICATION

Lilly had been very ill throughout her infancy and had been nursed for feeding as well as for comfort well into her second year. She did not have a transitional object nor was she especially attached to any one of her many soft toys. But mother and Lilly often played with them, which both enjoyed thoroughly. Lilly transferred her ability to initiate and pursue symbolic play to Toddler Group rather soon. She used the kitchen corner to serve meals and often accepted teachers as well as peers into her "parties," but she also used the animals, cars, blocks, and staged elaborate sequences. Sometimes she created happy occasions, sometimes she enacted things that had scared her or made her angry. Sometimes she compensated for having felt inferior or incompetent by staging a game in which her pretend representative was the biggest and could boss everyone. Mother could always tune in, understand, and enjoy.

Marjorie had not only been ill but inadequately cared for during infancy and began to relate, enjoy need-fulfillment, and develop functions in the latter part of her second year with the help of her foster mother. Marjorie did not have a transitional object or favorite toy. She did not play at all. Once she brought a doll she had received as a gift to show us, but she had no name for it, and it was soon set aside in her cubby. It had value as a present, not as a symbol.

Since Marjorie made no progress with playing at home or in Toddler Group, we eventually invited her and her mother to a pretend meal. At first she only sat close to mother and watched her and us enjoy our "dinner." Then she herself became active and began to serve meals. Eventually she took two dolls, put them in mother's lap, and asked her to give them the food she had prepared. Mom lovingly held, fed, and talked for them, serving as intermediary. In time, Marjorie used this play to create sequences from her own life, inviting or rejecting dolls, and sometimes teachers. She initiated a similar game in the sandbox. The first time a peer invited her to eat his sandpies she was thrilled and took the spoonful of sand home to keep. She branched out in her play, and initiated and participated in many imaginary games during her nursery school years. We learned at that time that Marjorie still treasured the spoonful of sand and referred to it as "That's the first pie Jimmy gave me."

We could even help those toddlers play who, with or without a transitional object, had suffered overwhelming early experiences and therefore either could not use symbols for fear of getting out of control or who started to play but quickly got overwhelmed with excitement or aggression.

Zachary had no transitional object and used his pacifier not to comfort himself but to plug his mouth. His kitchen play always deteriorated into a jumble of dishes and aggressive pretend gobbling, and the little cars on his road always ended up bashing each other and nearby real people. His mother sat by helpless and uninvolved or anxiously trying to direct him, the pitch of her voice rising as her worry and anger increased. We told Zachary that we could see he so much wanted to have a nice safe game but something got in the way and we would therefore try to help. With mother participating, we limited the number of dishes or cars to reduce the stimulation, asked Zachary about his plan, such as "all the cars have to drive home," and helped him implement it. When things threatened to get out of control, we sometimes introduced a containing element; for example, when a car started to career off course, the teacher's car would catch up with it, tell the driver that he was not safe, that Zachary had really wanted him to drive home, and that our driver would accompany him to help him. Zachary's reckless driver usually accepted help and Zachary was delighted when he could complete his game in a contained way. Of course, Zachary was helped with his troubles by his mother at other times, but her and our assistance with playing made a contribution and afforded him a chance to experience inner mastery. Feeling safe increased his pleasure in playing, and the more he could trust himself, the more he could use play to express himself.

But we could not help all children to play and our failure proved most instructive.

Walter was a wanted child who had always enjoyed good health. He did not have a transitional object, though he possibly used his continuing night-time bottle in this fashion. In Toddler Group, from the latter half of his second year on, he sometimes sucked on his fingers at times of stress. More often he used mother's body for comfort, for excitement, and to mistreat. Mother also used his body, snuggling or caressing it, and sometimes holding or pushing him a bit roughly without considering his wishes or level of stimulation. When he ate her food or spat it out into her hand, as well as when she reached into his mouth to retrieve some food she did not want him to eat, their lack of bodily differentiation was striking. Even more striking were other aspects of mother's relating with Walter as with a part of herself. She encouraged or interfered with his self-care, depending on her need of the moment, and in the same way, she cared for him or handed him over without considering his feelings. She adored him and fought for special privileges for him, but more often than not she dismissed or denied his considerable difficulties. Even the help she did give him served more to protect her sufficiently from having her pride hurt and tended to fall short of meeting his need.

As in all these areas, there was little real communication between mother and child and none in symbolic form. Mother claimed Walter played a lot at home with his somewhat older cousin and his father. In Toddler Group there was no play. Despite many efforts, we could not enlist mother in playing with Walter and he could not pick up on the teachers' repeated attempts to enlist him. He could copy what we did but that was all. When father visited and witnessed one of these abortive, compliant, but joyless occasions, he was concerned and related how play went at home. With father and cousin, play consisted mostly of boisterous superman-type enactments but, even when it was less excited and aggressive, the initiative and ideas were never Walter's. He just copied or did as he was told. Thus, in their play, as with mother, Walter met the needs of others to maintain their self-oriented investment in him but never asserted himself as a person in his own right. In play, as in other areas, he leaned on them to supply his self-regard but had no inner resources to draw on. During his nursery years, his teachers' help with play and with just being his own person were also limited. He was a compliant partner in the play of others and willingly learned the tasks adults set before him, but there was no initiative or creativity.

Reflecting on our sad experience with Walter helped us to understand better why our interventions made a difference with the other children. It confirmed for us that the child's beginning differentiation from mother and capacity to "create" a meaningful transitional object has to be matched by a parallel development in the mother's relationship with her child. Without her reciprocal ability to understand and communicate via this early play, his efforts wither. The transitional object is then either not created or fails to lead to later forms of play. However, the transitional object is not the most essential element. Play may start even without a transitional object when mother and child reach the appropriate level between unity and differentiation in their relationship, and become capable of communicating in symbolic form. In these instances, either partner may initiate the dialogue. The child always signals his readiness with pretend (i.e., symbolic) maternal caretaking, and the mother's initiative tends to take the same form. For this reason, we as teachers preferred this line of approach but succeeded only when we could involve mother because play *is* communication with mother at first.

In our Toddler Group, boys and girls began by feeding mother or doll most often. Some combined it with comforting, putting to bed to sleep, holding and rocking, dressing, or carrying. Mothers' faces usually light up with pleasure when they see this and they at once join in with words, participating action, or rapt attention as they mentally accompany and share in their child's activity. They are drawn to it as if by a magnet, and this is equally true of the child's response when mother, or mother and teacher, initiate the play. The intense yet calm, almost awed pleasure as mother and child focus on these first discoveries of play is hard to describe. As teachers we look on in respectful, hushed silence, grateful to be there to witness it. The experience comes closest perhaps to seeing a mother and father holding and gazing at their newborn, a feel of, "This is me and you but, above all, a thing we created with a life of its own which is a new bond between us."

Once it has come to be, play usually soon either leaves the theme of maternal caretaking or adds new themes, and in either case, becomes more elaborate, but its progress depends on the continuation of mutual symbolic understanding. Just how long this dependence is essential is an open question.

> With Lilly, for example, whose play had progressed and branched out so well, there was a period during her first nursery school year, when she created experiences the mother could not understand and/or accept, and she disinvested Lilly's play, although the latter made many overtures. Lilly then gave up playing, withdrew into fantasies, and during the next two years did not progress to creativity with drawing, painting, sculpting as several other toddlers did. Instead, she appeared to focus on regaining mother's involvement in other ways, most prominently via bodily care. She eventually transferred this in part to asking for and taking care of pets and in this activity she could reengage mother who shared Lilly's interest, helped with it, and sensed its importance as a bond between them. By that time it contained elements of the family threesome.

In other cases where mother cannot share in the mutual symbolic communication, play can get stuck, become repetitive, and devoid of creative pleasure. We observe this most poignantly in many day care centers. There the most well-integrated toddlers play maternal caretaking endlessly in a serious, almost driven manner. They leave this play reluctantly when they have to, and return to it as soon as they get the chance.

There is no mother to share with. Some caregivers regard this as nice play, although they may complain about the children's difficulty in leaving it. The more thoughtful caregivers show concern over its monotony and self-absorption. As a consultant, I often suggest that the caregiver not only join the play but empathize verbally about how hard it is not to have mother share in it, that they will tell mother at pick-up time how much she was missed, and how nice it would be if they could play this game together on home days. When mother can then be helped to "tune in," the play with the caregiver becomes a sufficient bridge for progression.

LEARNING

Learning, like playing, involves mother and toddler in an endeavor which is the shared focus of their relationship; in other words, they do not look at each other but at the process at hand. As with playing too, the initiative may start with either partner but presupposes a parallel readiness in both to make fruitful participation possible, to engender calm pleasure, to motivate each to go on to new and more complex endeavors, and to respond to each other's next "moves." And of course the first learning, like the first play, tends to revolve around maternal caretaking, learning to do for oneself—the tasks of self-care which take up so much of our learning curriculum in Toddler Group. Learning in this sense is never an interaction in which the adult teaches and the child learns, much less one in which the teacher simply decides what the child has to learn, but a shared undertaking to which both contribute, and in many ways, both learn. There are, for example, no two youngsters who approach even a simple wooden puzzle in the same way, and when one can persuade a mother to discover and support her child's own thinking process instead of imposing her way, she can enjoy the learning as much as he does.

However, there are also many differences between playing and learning (E. Furman, 1969c, 1985a, 1986, 1987). The pursuit and outcome of learning always deals with reality, whereas play remains in the world of illusion. Also, although neither play nor learning provide direct need or impulse gratification, the shared focus on a goal-directed task in learning requires much more available neutral energy, much more frustration tolerance and impulse control. And not least, the teacher–pupil relationship, though derived from the relationship with the mother-as-teacher, becomes a very special function- and time-limited relationship, while playing with peers and adults retains the features of mutual symbolic understanding that were the essence of the earlier mother–child play.

In describing our educational approach and goals (chapter 2), I detailed the many ways in which we assist mother and toddler with mutually responsive teaching-learning and gradually build the beginnings of a teacher–pupil relationship between ourselves and the child. In relation to self-care, for example, we start with the mother getting in tune with her child's readiness, recognizing and appreciating his wish to learn, and assisting him with the steps in mastery, from doing for to doing with, to standing by to admire and ultimate independent know-how. Throughout, we help by supporting the change from pleasure in bodily gratification to pleasure in mastery, from immediate to delayed satisfaction, from fun in doing what comes easily to pride in trying and improving little by little. The first teacher-initiated activities are built on the ones mother and child have usually shared at home or, at least, mother has been doing them and the child has wanted to do them with her and like her—cleaning tables, pouring juice, making pudding, baking cookies.

FROM READING WITH MOTHER TO ENJOYING BOOKS

Even the loved, mother–child invested activities, however, have to overcome major hurdles before they serve real learning with a teacher, especially in a group setting.

A familiar example is reading books, which most toddlers are reported to love. Many indeed readily transfer this loved activity to Toddler Group, either choose a book to read with mother or gladly accept her offer. They are usually calm and comfortable during this period. Close observation shows, however, that their enjoyment of "reading books" derives from many different sources. The child may simply be cuddled up close and using mother's voice as soothing background music; the child may be holding the book, flipping the pages, and doing most of the talking, or naming all the things mother points to. Regardless, it is the mother–child togetherness that really matters. The story is a vehicle for interaction but means little of itself. This becomes glaringly evident when the same toddler is asked to sit alongside others in a small semicircle to listen to a story read by a teacher. Some withdraw, sucking their thumbs; some "wiggle," fall off their chairs or roll on the floor. Some need a drink or want to use the toilet, are cold, hot, or want to sit on the reader's lap, and almost all want the story just for themselves, move up close, and obscure the view for others, which leads to cries of "I can't see" and pokes and pushes. Many children want to touch and hold the book, to see and hear the story, to use all their senses at the same time. Even much later, in nursery school and beyond, story time is often not much different, with perhaps less manifest clamor but not much more interest in the content of the book. Teachers always try to disregard this and hope that the really interesting or exciting story and skilled presentation of it will override these interferences. This is not the case. Using books to learn from and for aesthetic enjoyment requires major preparatory masteries, and these have to be learned with the help of mother and teacher. Many mothers sense this. Even though they rightly say that their toddler loves reading with them, when we prepare them for our circle time, they respond with, "Oh dear, he'll never sit and pay attention."

In our Toddler Group each mother sits with her child in the semicircle of our "rug time" so that their book-reading togetherness can be included to an extent, that needs can be met, should they arise, and that mother can participate in and support the steps in learning. We start with ten minutes and gradually extend the period to fifteen. We start with one picture, add a second, and then a third on successive days. We start with simple familiar themes, such as food items and a series of a child sleeping, washing, eating breakfast. The actual time for showing and understanding the pictures takes at first but a couple of minutes, with the rest of the period spent on activity songs, which are much easier because they involve movement and singing of rhymes. Even so, the same behaviors take place as described in the story hour above. This is where the learning starts. As each opportunity arises, we talk about what a big boy and girl job it is to look without touching, how hard to stay in one's own place with mommy so everyone can see, to keep one's legs still and in one's own space so they don't bother others. We tell them we shall practice all this, and in time they will learn it and feel good about it. We often stop to recognize and appreciate a special effort or small success, the mothers help with their support, and the children beam. With increasing pleasure and achievement in self-control, the interest in the pictures begins to exceed the need for the earlier bodily gratifications. We can then introduce themes from the wider but still familiar world (pets, farm animals, birds), and short books, basking in the much discussed delight of being ready for such an advance. Eventually we graduate to themes and stories which provide altogether new information, new symbolic understanding, and the ability to empathize with fictional characters, in short the stuff that books are all about. Needless to say, this real liking of books is achieved toward the end of the year, even then only partially, and always carefully linked to the children's life and other learning experiences, e.g., *The Carrot Seed* (Krauss, 1945). This is a relatively long sequence with a mixture of realistic and symbolic elements. It can be enjoyed and understood, intellectually and with feeling, only in the context of many months of experience with planting and growing, with its failures and successes, frustrations and joys.

THE TOOLS OF MASTERY

The process of learning to use books is much like learning about other things. The example of the books stressed the teacher's and mother's role in valuing frustration tolerance and mastery, in making the pursuit and least attainment of them a matter of pleasurable pride, in order to facilitate the transition from bodily gratification to neutral pleasure. And it stressed also the importance of working toward integration of the contents, the subject matter. In both these areas the mother's attitude and participation are crucial for the toddler. The relationship with the teacher is too tenuous to affect these difficult developmental steps on its own. When mother's and teacher's approaches are at odds, the child's loyalty conflict is exacerbated and draws learning into its orbit to such an extent as to make it prohibitively conflictual.

> Jason, well developed and intelligent, started his outdoor play by pushing a tricycle. Mother confirmed that he liked to do that at home. When I wondered whether it would not be more fun to learn to ride it, mother looked surprised, and did not think he was ready. But Jason was quite eager to get on it. Mother then pushed the trike. I again suggested it might be more fun to make it go himself. He tried and succeeded at once, but did not steer. I said I would help with that and he would learn that too. In the meantime he could work on his peddling. He did and whenever it got a bit hard he responded to my enthusiastic support of what a good job he was doing and how good it feels when one tries hard, even if it doesn't work well right away. Mother said nothing.
>   The next time Jason again pushed the trike and mother just walked along. She continued to walk along with the same lack of affect when he changed to riding it, but he gave up very quickly, and without visible feeling, even though I reminded him how happy he had been when he had worked hard at it and done such a good job. This sequence repeated itself in all areas, learning to push on the see-saw as opposed to being pushed, learning to sit at rug time as opposed to rolling on the floor, learning to use the scissors, to roll out playdough. In each instance, Jason's easily sparked interest subsided with mother's evident lack of shared pleasure and support. It took the mother a long time to become aware of her difficulty, and then to understand and overcome her reluctance to support his becoming an active independent boy. When she finally could support him, he could fortunately still respond.

Some mothers experience no pleasure in mastery themselves, and in regard to their toddler, want him "just to have fun." They feel that any expectation of effort is an imposition and will spoil the fun. They are surprised to hear that working toward and achieving mastery provide a different kind of fun and are amazed to find their child thrilled with what he wants to and can do. Sometimes his delight helps them change their attitude. Sometimes they can identify with the teacher's pleasure in supporting his mastering. Sometimes they even realize that they had always really wanted to master but had not known how or had not trusted they could do it. Now they feel they can pick up and move ahead with their child, and, of course, with the support of teacher and therapist.

> Linda stuck to the simplest activities, and even then often enlisted mother's help or failed to complete them. Faced with the least obstacle, challenge, or mistake, she lost interest and gave up. "It's not fun." Mother would have wanted Linda to do well but she did not want to "pressure" her, and beyond a few half-hearted admonitions, quietly complied, and usually ended up with Linda sitting on her lap being read to. Like Linda, mother wanted to do well but looking helpless, said she didn't know what to do, it was just so hard.
>
> Our first chance came with playing roll-a-ball. Linda was rolling the ball along aimlessly, but responded to the teacher's invitation to roll it back and forth, with mother as our partner. The first balls rolled every which way, but Linda persisted with the teacher's encouragement and promise of mastery, and all three of us cheered and had fun with the first, probably accidental success. We played roll-a-ball each time. Linda began to aim the ball zestfully and with some glee, and she happily reported on her efforts and fun to dad at home. We began to make the game harder, little by little, eventually played catch, and Linda herself initiated shooting baskets. The greatest thrill, however, was mother's, "I never had so much fun."
>
> For some time each activity followed this course: teacher's support of child and mother, mother engaging herself as a child, both of them learning to learn and have fun mastering. One time, as Linda and mother were happily busy painting napkin rings for a dinner occasion at home, mother suddenly said: "Nobody ever did this with me when I was little. I didn't know how to do these things. I didn't know they could be so much fun." Mother's ability to use her child's growth to grow herself helped

her and Linda in many areas—an experience shared by several mothers.

Some mothers are very intent on their child achieving but they can only "make him," instruct him in a controlling way, instead of supporting pleasure in mastery. Some have to impose their means of mastering, unable to trust their child's capacities. They are unable to appreciate that one part of the pleasure in learning consists of the child figuring out his own ways, enjoying exercising his own functions. This does not mean that the child may not need help, but help in assessing and reassessing how his approach is working out or how he might alter or improve it, not help by being told, "This is the way to do it." This kind of language often implies, "This is my way, the only way, and you have to accept it without thinking for yourself." This comes up not only with puzzles, as I mentioned earlier, but with every bit of learning, be it how to draw a face, how to hang up a jacket, how to handle scissors.

Another way of looking at the question of how and when to help with learning is in terms of gauging the child's readiness to integrate help; for example, at which point in his thinking can he integrate a suggestion, when is it helpful for him to compare his approach with that of others, how do we word advice so as to further rather than disrupt his efforts.

LEARNING AND INTEGRATION

The ability to integrate affects all aspects of learning as well as of teaching. This applies to methodology and content, as was illustrated with the example of reading books, as well as to extending one area of learning into many other parts of the curriculum. The latter was illustrated with the earlier example of dressing (chapter 2), where learning to put on outdoor clothes was related to a whole array of related activities. It applies, above all, to learning in such a way that it makes sense, facilitates the understanding of an entire process, and relates concrete observation to the use of symbols. This promotes the wish to figure out how things work and the trust that it can be done. In contrast to the widely held belief that young children enjoy magic and fantasy because it fits in with their self-centered omnipotent thinking, our experiences indicate that these preferences are often substitutes for the lack of understanding of the world around them, which leaves children helpless and confused. The thirst for and delight with opportunities for real understanding afford ample proof. No magic tale about the heavens or an intriguing song like "Twinkle, Twinkle Little Star" brings the deep satisfaction that comes from finding one's first real star in the evening sky. By the same token, getting to know one part of the process, however much fun it may be, does not compare with coming to understand the whole, from beginning to end. Buying peas at the store provides nothing like the pleasure that planting and harvesting one's own does, and then saving some of the peas and watching them produce the next crop; in short, understanding the life cycle. The work, the waiting, even the attendant frustrations are well worth it, not because homegrown peas taste better (though they do!), but because the undertaking affords total understanding.

The usual activities in toddler as well as in preschool classes do not meet these criteria. Craft projects, such as caterpillars made out of egg cartons, or songs such as "Baa, Baa, Black Sheep," mean nothing to children who have rarely if ever seen a caterpillar or a sheep. Worse yet, these activities do not foster their wanting to see or know about real caterpillars and sheep. As described earlier (chapter 2), our curriculum focuses as much as possible on helping the children to observe and make sense of their environment, to understand its why's and how's, the causal connections and time sequences which support logical thinking, and provide for integrated as opposed to fragmented learning. The mainstay of this approach is our learning about the life cycle with plants (E. Furman, 1990). Using familiar foods, for example sweet potatoes, we start with items which grow fast in water so that root and leaf growth can be clearly followed. We then proceed to plants which still grow fast but out of direct view for a short period; for example, the children shell corn cobs and plant the kernels, which soon sprout. They plant beans in jars with moist paper towels, and then after they have sprouted put the beans into pots with earth to produce blooms and pods. As spring approaches, we are ready to grow green onions, peas, and potatoes in our tiny vegetable garden. All along, we all collect, compare, and plant other seeds, from apples, oranges, and grapefruits to acorns, hickory nuts, and pine seeds shaken out of pine cones. These observations with growing are matched by observations of dying, the ways plants wilt, decay, and are buried to decompose and enrich the soil. All this is fascinating to our toddlers who previously have followed these processes only from the store to the dining table or trash can. They quickly extend their understanding to other forms of living and dying, the small animals, the insects and worms they find, and the bigger animals, such as the squirrels who nest in the trees or are found killed by the side of the road. Occasionally this knowledge prepares them for coping with death which also involves a personal loss, such as the passing of a pet or of a grandparent. They also begin to observe and question different life forms, pointing out mushrooms on the bark of trees, bringing shells they found or onions which had sprouted in the bag in mother's kitchen drawer.

The thrill of "It can make sense" is fully shared by the mothers. Most of them too did not know how peas or potatoes grow, where popcorn comes from, that galls are insect nurseries. They too begin to look at daily foods and common sights with different eyes, want to know why and how. Instead of seeking out programs and performances to entertain their youngsters, they start going for walks, find farms to visit, orchards to pick fruit, and a spot in their yard to grow some vegetables.

Earlier (chapter 9) I described what happens when we are unable to spark the mother's enthusiasm for this kind of learning or when she is unable to support extending it to other areas. For example, the child can suffer speechless bewilderment when mother refers to a buried rotten sweet potato as "nicely sleeping," or he can get lost in a maze of misconstrued concerns when she is unable to help him extend his knowledge about the death of plants and animals to the death of his grandmother. The seemingly independent, self-motivated pleasure in integrating knowledge then falters in the face of mother's different attitude, and the teacher's only way of bringing it back is by reenlisting mother's support. Whereas the older child and, to an extent, even the preschooler, can sustain his own pleasure in understanding with the help of the relationship with a teacher, the toddler's efforts depend directly on the mother.

When a subject, such as the theme of the life cycle, is introduced by the teacher to mother and child, successful learning and integration of it require two conditions. The first is reciprocity, the teacher offers to share an interest, then picks up on the aspect they respond to, and then, step by step through mutual give and take, allows the content to develop along the lines indicated by this interaction. For example, when planting outdoors, the child's interest may focus on the composition of the soil or on the bugs he finds in it, rather than on the seeds to be planted. Such child-initiated interests have led to fascinating shared discoveries and have enriched rather than interfered with the teacher's approach or plan. Above all, they have demonstrated what the child perceived as an integrated learning experience and enabled him to make it his own, whereas the teacher's plan would have constituted an imposition and fragmentation of his process. Of course, the teacher's and mother's willingness to learn from and with him often prompts his willingness to learn with them.

This brings us to the second condition, namely that the teacher can helpfully offer to share only what she herself thoroughly enjoys. She has to impart not only knowledge but enthusiasm. Learning has to be made pleasurable, not by making it exciting for the child, but by conveying the teacher's own love of it. This is the most important contribution of the relationship with the teacher. For the very young child especially, no toy, no skill, and certainly no sustained learning activity truly engages him in and of itself. They only become meaningful when mother and teacher work at it with him because they enjoy it (not because they want him to like it, learn it, or occupy himself with it). And here again, the teacher's pleasure in learning about something she likes has to match the mother's pleasure or be imparted to her. Without her pleasure, the child's may be limited to the class period, but fails to become an integrated part of his growing personality. Using the relationship to make learning pleasurable is especially important with toddlers, in part because it helps them to acquire this "new taste," and in part because their own attitudes are still so predominantly fueled by primitive urge-related energy that they readily cause inner conflict and hence interference. I noted examples of this earlier; how often toddlers' excited looking leads to not looking; how their mouth urges and conflict about them extends to all forms of taking in and leads to an inability to take in suggestions or explanations; how their concerns over bodily inferiority spread to every kind of "performance" and manifest themselves in pervasive restrictions.

Following our toddlers' progress, we found that their interest and pleasure in learning remained with them and enabled them to benefit from later teaching in all instances where it had been possible to engage them and their mothers. In some cases it faltered under stress, but was recouped after the stress subsided. In two cases particularly, however, we could not engage the mother's pleasure or support. These youngsters still learned later quite well in class but their learning remained dependent on the relationship with the teacher, failed to become integrated, and did not serve as a self-motivating force.

This highlights a serious concern for toddlers in day care. However dedicated and knowledgeable the teacher–caregiver may be, the mothers are usually not involved in the child's learning, and even when the center tries to share information, the opportunities for this are limited. The children's learning then has little chance of becoming a part of their personality. Thus we often see in our consulting work with day care centers that a child learned well with his caregiver, but cannot apply himself later in public school.

SOCIALIZING

Most of our toddlers had older siblings, and a few had younger ones. All had been with other children, in the wider families, neighborhood, and in other toddler groups, with or without their mothers. Some parents reported how well their toddler got along with others or how aggressive he was with them, or how aggressive they were with him. With several cases, the mistreatment suffered at the hands of an older brother or sister or the child's own marked aggression to peers were the main reasons for referral to our Toddler Group. The parents predicted on this basis that their toddler would be very fearful and unable to defend himself or that he would be a menace to his classmates. As mentioned earlier, these predictions did not materialize, and other reported behaviors with peers also did not manifest themselves in the Toddler Group, or could be seen in a very different light. The main reasons for many of these differences included, of course, the fact that the siblings were not present, that each child had his mother with him, and that mothers and teachers adhered to our rule of "everyone and everything has to be very safe." This provided ongoing protection for each child against inner and outer dangers. Thus, when the aggressively mistreated toddlers showed no fear and stood up for themselves, and those who had aggressively mistreated others ceased their attacks, it was clearly related to their feeling safe. This was because they knew that mother would not leave them at the unpredictable mercy of others, or of their own impulses, but was fully invested and would intervene on their behalf. We often observed how quickly the children's behavior reverted to what the parents had reported whenever we saw them in the hall, waiting room, or parking lot, and when mother no longer protected them. She might be chatting with other mothers, might be unable to invest both her children (e.g., focusing on the older one but "losing" the younger one), or could not remain in charge without the teachers' support and expectation. Many mothers could be helped to recognize this as their difficulty, worked on it in treatment-via-the-parent, and succeeded in overcoming it sufficiently. Some were less aware, or less successful, and the differences between their children's home and school behavior persisted to a greater extent.

The "they get along so well" behaviors took longer to understand and were individually more varied.

Abe was reported to maintain close and predominantly loving relationships with his slightly older brothers with whom he liked to play and who always included him. They were said to be such good friends that they often wanted to sleep together, and sometimes did. In Toddler Group Abe stayed very close to his mother, included the teachers as he got to know us, but never reached out to other children. He was aware of them, however. This showed primarily in his not joining in activities or practicing skills when they were engaged in the same pursuits or when he thought they were looking at him. Also, when someone asked him to share his toy or give up part of his space, Abe always readily surrendered to their request. We thought Abe felt intimidated and inferior, but mother considered him kind and overlooked his restriction. When we played "Here We Go Round the Mulberry Bush" Abe became quite upset and fearful. Mother clarified for him that it would be different than when he played this with his brothers. It turned out they got quite excited and rough and Abe often ended up at the bottom of the pile as they climaxed the game by jumping on top of one another. Reassured, Abe joined us and enjoyed the game. Another time Abe's brother joined us for a little while in Toddler Group as his Dad was late picking him up. The brother quickly finished the activity he had been given, and instead of asking for more material to work with, took over Abe's, belittled his efforts, and wedged himself between Abe and mother. Abe looked more and more unhappy and withdrawn. It was only when the teachers intervened by pointing this out to mother that Abe subtly pushed his brother, and then, with mother's help, regained his seat next to her. On yet another occasion Abe had wet himself just after leaving Toddler Group. Mother handled this very kindly with Abe on this as on prior occasions, but she was oblivious to the fact that his brother, awaiting him at the door with an aunt, dressed Abe down mercilessly and made him cringe with humiliation. Undoubtedly there were also times when the brothers were nice or, particularly, when they mothered him, but the mother had denied the unkind interactions and Abe's response, though they took place in her presence.

We had several toddlers whose parents, for various reasons, could not recognize that their child's "getting along so well" with others, be they siblings or peers, in fact entailed helpless compliance with harsh mistreatment, arbitrary rejections, and excited overstimulation.

Some mothers misinterpreted their toddler's behavior in a different way, thinking, for instance, that his impulse to take others' things in preference to his own or imitating another's behavior, represented his wish to play with them. Some mothers had taken their children already as infants to various groups because they felt they needed to provide opportunities for company and peer play, but they were oblivious to their child's bewilderment and stress at finding himself surrounded by a noisy and incomprehensible hubbub. We saw this reaction with a few of our toddlers who entered after such experiences. But it is in evidence even more often and more markedly with other youngsters who had been in day care through toddlerhood, and later got bewildered or out of control in any group situation the moment everyone was not occupied with a uniform structured activity. Transitions, outdoor play, and free play confused and overstimulated them.

On entry to Toddler Group, our toddlers paid no heed to their peers and certainly showed no inclination to interact with them in a friendly manner, regardless of whether their prior experiences with other children had been reported to be good or bad. They often did not know their classmates' names for some time and did not notice when one of them was absent. Since each had his mother with him, there was no rivalry for mother's love or attention and, until they had built a meaningful relationship with us, there was no rivalry over the teachers' attention. The toddlers' attitudes to competing or not competing over toys and materials reflected a similar lack of real caring for their peers as people. Many were from the start preoccupied with what others had, and often enough, this was the very thing they wanted. Had we not interfered, they would have forcefully grabbed whatever toy another was using or intruded into his space to take over his activity, all without as much as looking at the other child, much less considering his feelings. We learned in time that those youngsters who exhibited this behavior to an extreme had very low self-esteem and were unable to enjoy anything the moment it was theirs. But we also found that those who at first did not go for others' things and seemed very content to occupy themselves with a toy for a long time, did not really play constructively. Rather, they were used to having everything snatched from them, usually by an older sibling, were too intimidated to protest, and simply hung on to the one toy they had, wondering, as it were, how soon they would have to surrender it.

A couple of older toddlers at first surprised us by their seeming kindness. When another child threatened to intrude, they quickly gave him a part of their toy, such as a couple of pegs. This, it turned out, was an acceptable way to appease a younger sibling and mother and was counterbalanced by their being especially "grabby" in other situations, such as trying to use three shovels in the sandbox and all the pails. Similarly, a toddler's caring for and about another child, as we sometimes see in day care settings, represents the former child's need for being mothered rather than a response to the need of the latter, and is often forcefully imposed when the "baby" no longer wants to be "mothered."

In one area, however, peers mattered a great deal and that was when one of them manifested an intense feeling—anger, sadness, fear, and excitement. Some just stared, some questioned it anxiously, some immediately imitated it. Less overt but all the more profound was their concern over a difference which they perceived as "something's wrong." This included bodily anomalies, such as an injury or slightly spastic gait, as well as unfamiliar characteristics, such as a different skin color or facial features. In all these instances, the other child represented a threat; not a threat of being attacked, as might be the case with another's angry outburst, but a threat borne of lack of differentiation and vulnerability of the self. It implied "This is me. This will overtake me. This will erase my fragile sense of bodily and mental integrity."

The mothers were often as unaware of their child's difficulty with differentiation from peers in some situations as they were of his lack of appreciating them as equal people in other situations. Actually, both aspects highlight the fact that effective empathy with others and the wish to interact with them as equals presupposes feeling sufficiently secure as an individual and sufficiently safe from inner and outer dangers.

Randy, close to 2 years old, was prepared for having fun playing with two slightly older youngsters during a family get-together. The mother was present to supervise the play but expected

Randy to be a nice host and share his toys. Randy complied but became increasingly tense and unhappy, sitting apart while they used his toys. That night he called out desperately in his sleep "Mine, mine." The parents realized that their expectation of his sharing had made him feel unsafe, and when they talked with Randy about it, he told them he never wanted to play with anyone again. When the next occasion for a child's visit came up, they prepared Randy differently. They asked him to select a couple of toys he felt he could temporarily spare for the guest to use, assured him they would help him keep all his other toys off-limits, and promised to spend most of the time at a nearby playground, where both children could use the ample equipment and where the other mother would accompany them to attend to her child while Randy's mom would be there to help him. The visit went off well. There was even some parallel play on the swings, and Randy showed his interest in the guest by later sharing several observations and questions about him.

In our Toddler Group we very much encourage peer relations by helping the children feel safe from and with their classmates. To start with, each child is reassured by his mother's invested presence; but this alone is not enough. We are alert to the toddlers' concerns about differentiating themselves, and we address these, via the mother if at all possible, so that she can say, "Yes, Johnny is having a very angry (or sad) time, but his Mommy is helping him and it is not your trouble"; or, "Yes, Mary does have a bandage to help make her sore arm better. Her Mommy took her to their doctor and he said the bandage would help and her arm will soon be all right again. It's too bad and I'm sorry for Mary, but I am also glad that you are fine and we'll make sure you stay safe." Once the child is helped to feel separate and safe, he can then ask and understand more about the causes of an injury in a calm way, whereas such questions prior to feeling safe tend to be anxiously insistent and answers cannot be listened to or are used as a substitute for reassurance. Sometimes the mother cannot assure and explain because she is not in feeling touch with her child and the teacher has to take the initiative with mother and child. This happened in the example described earlier (chapter 2), where Mary and Marjorie were, unbeknownst to their mothers, deeply affected by their responses to the other's different skin color.

Another way we help with feeling safe is to make sure that nobody gets hurt by another, and nobody intrudes on another's space or play, or takes something from him without asking and waiting for the other child's reply. Although we value and appreciate kindness, we make sure that each child knows he can say "no" to another, and that his refusal of a request will be honored. When we stop a child from hurting or imposing on a peer, we clarify the advantage of our general safety rule for him—how could he feel safe and be sure we would protect him from others if we let him hurt them? When the relationship with the mother, supported by the teacher, provides full protection and respect, when she is able to convey her own attitudes of empathic interest in others as well as value and appreciate them in her child, he can begin to think of and feel with other children. This achievement precedes the later wish to interact with them. At first we see merely the acknowledgment of peers as people in their own right, by listening to what they say at the snack table, noticing which cubby belongs to whom, remembering their names, asking about a child who is absent, being aware of when another uses the bathroom. Of course, we recognize and value each of these little steps and support them by singing songs which include the children's names, or have them notice what color clothes they are wearing, or by making cards for absentees which each child may "sign" with his color symbol.

Next we begin to see acts of kindness. When they know that another child is waiting for a turn with the toy they are using, they often spontaneously bring it to him after finishing with it. Or when they notice that a peer is looking for a piece of a toy that rolled out of sight, they find and give it to him. Sometimes the mere knowledge that they can refuse a request, such as exchanging sandbox pails or using part of the doll dishes, allows them to agree to it and feel good about being so kind. Occasionally we see evidence of improved differentiation quite clearly; for example, when one little girl, who had been very upset by others' anger, watched a boy yelling angrily, she suddenly said, "I am not Jimmy," and felt relieved, and able to continue her own activity.

PEERS AS PEOPLE

Very gradually others are sought out as companions. The seesaw is often a good indicator of this. At first the children want to sit on it alone, with mother helping them hold on, and they accept the teacher sitting at the other end only to make it go up and down. As we accompany this activity with the familiar song of "Seesaw, Marjorie Daw," it is soon a favorite, and they then allow another child to sit at the other end, with the teacher standing in the middle, singing and helping it move. But the other child might as well be a rock for all the attention he gets, and, were it not for us, they would get off the seesaw suddenly without a thought of what this would do to the safety of their partner. But gradually they begin to look for a child to join them, at first any child, then a particular child, and the up-and-down pumping is enjoyed for the happy interaction. They now watch how the other one goes up when they are down, delight in making it happen, call to each other laughingly, and say "done" to prepare him for dismounting. The partner may then show real disappointment, beg for another turn, and may even get it, just to please. Similarly, "tea parties" in the kitchen corner or sandbox are enjoyed together, they invite and serve each other, sometimes even considerately asking which food the other child wants, and obliging him by perhaps making a new "chocolate" sand pie instead of the "cherry" pie they had prepared. They now say hello and goodbye to one another, sometimes with a special hug. They show each other their new shoes, a new haircut, or even a picture or block building they made. The peer's opinion matters: "Karen is my friend." Sometimes children help each other out when the adults cannot; for example, two boys, both with markedly unclear speech, accurately "translated" for one another when neither mothers nor teachers could understand one of them—a mutual kindness each child greatly appreciated, in the giving and in the receiving of it.

Of course, these developments are not only the result of our educational measures. As the year goes on, the toddlers' personalities mature in many areas, but by comparison with other settings, we find that considerate socializing comes about earlier in our Toddler Group and stands them in good stead during later phases. In particular, it helps to modify and over-come the many negatives which are an inevitable part of real relationships. Once the other children are viewed as people, and especially as concerns about bodily differences and ade-quacy intensify age-appropriately, peers become ready targets for rivalry, envy, and competition, both in their own right and by way of displacement from feelings about the parents. Build-ing with blocks in parallel play may turn into a race of whose is the tallest tower; choosing the next harder puzzle may be motivated by wanting to outdo a peer whose progress with puzzles has been closely watched. At circle time, one child may want to outshine all the others and at snack he may want to "out talk" them. Envy over a new hair ribbon may prompt a later rejection or refusal of a request. Rivalry over the teacher's attention can become intense, as may worries over getting left out. One boy, for whom this was especially acute, created a terrible fuss when he had to wait for his turn to get the apple slices I was preparing. His mother tried to calm and reassure him, to no avail. I finally asked: "Timmy, do you really think I would forget about you?" He stopped, thought, then his face burst into a smile as he replied, "No, you wouldn't." Sharing can indeed become very hard.

One time Alan hogged all the playdough. When another child wanted to use some too, Alan carefully broke off a little crumb and gave it to him. His mother reprimanded him and wanted to take away his playdough to break it in half, but she desisted. Instead, we told Alan that we understood sharing was hard, but we also knew that he wanted to be a kind boy and would feel good if he could share enough so that the other child could also make things with the dough. We waited for a good ten minutes while Alan struggled with himself, passing on little bit by little bit. The other child waited patiently, obviously empathizing with Alan's conflict and effort, as did all the grown-ups and several other children who crowded around watching in awed silence. Finally, Alan rightly felt that he had shared a sufficient amount. The children applauded spontaneously, the adults were re-lieved, and praised him, and Alan had never felt so good. Later he referred to it with pride several times, "Do you remember when I shared my playdough?"

The children's birthday parties throughout the year provide a useful developmental measure for gauging their progress. They start off having no recognition of the personal meaning to themselves and others of the birthday. They are perhaps overcome by envy and anger (either at having to share little "favors" with their peers or by not getting the birthday gift). But in the end there is shared happiness at being part of the occasion with zestful singing for the birthday child and pleasure in the giving and receiving. There are even spontaneous thank you's.

MISUSING PEERS

Once sufficiently differentiated from them, peers also begin to serve as targets for feelings or behaviors one would rather not own in oneself. It becomes possible to enjoy peers' manifest anger or excitement vicariously, to copy their misbehavior in order to ward off one's own impulses, or by way of disowning one's responsibility for them, to encourage or provoke them to be naughty instead of doing it oneself. All this is impossible as long as the boundaries between self and other are too labile. Similarly, peers now readily become the target of what ought to be self-criticism, so that when a child is unhappy about his own work, he may go around belittling others' efforts and achievements, or when he is worried about his aggressive impulses he may complain that another wants to hit him or topple his tower. By way of turning the tables, a child may reject others to ward off the pain of having felt rejected. In these situations it is important to intervene, to clarify the reality, and to help the child notice that his behavior or words get in his way and come perhaps from a worry his mommy can help him know and cope with. The mother may then wish to discuss the incident further with the teacher to clarify it for herself and, in our setting, is helped by the therapist to explore the underlying difficulty with her child. Most frequently, the "misuse" of peers is secondary to the child's conflicts within the family, especially with the parents; for example, it may feel safer to envy a peer than a mother or father, or to be angry at and belittle another child than to jeopardize one's good standing with the parents. Peer relationships are freed only when these issues are understood and coped with in the appropriate context.

During their nursery school and kindergarten years, our toddlers, like all other children, needed such help with interferences at different developmental stages, but their early pleasurable interest and interactions were an important ally in wanting to overcome difficulties and maintaining or reestablishing positive relationships with peers. Throughout the later years, the ex-toddlers had a special feeling for each other, shared memories, empathized and helped one another during hard times (not least during the adjustment to nursery school), and several of them became true friends, often overcoming early rivalries or misgivings about each other. When some of them years later left town or went to another school, there was great sadness and, in most cases, they kept in touch through home visits and even letters. At the same time, most of these youngsters were also able to make friends with new children and in new settings. Their parents' ongoing understanding, protection, and support played a major part in these achievements.

CHAPTER 11

Transition into Nursery School

During attendance in Toddler Group, many youngsters encountered special stresses such as illness and medical or surgical treatments, death, divorce, birth of siblings, not to mention the stresses engendered by their own personality growth and by their parents' various difficulties in helping them. During the latter part of Toddler Group, all of them also showed us that the elimination-focused urges of their toddler phase were diminishing, while impulses related to curiosity, showing off, and concerns over competition became more pronounced and intense, a major, welcome, developmental step. But whereas these external and internal events were either strictly individual or occurred in piecemeal fashion, with its characteristic overlapping and back and forth movement, the developmental task of entry into Nursery School was shared by all, encompassed a specific time period, and served as a framework for highlighting many if not all aspects of the personality in interaction. We anticipated, therefore, that observation of this developmental task would afford an opportunity to assess the individual child's achievements, his strengths and weaknesses, as well as to compare the children with those who enter our Nursery School without prior group experience or after experience in other settings. Moreover, we had studied the developmental

209

task of entry into nursery school for a long time. We were very familiar with its prerequisites in terms of personality functioning, with the many subtle manifestations of the child's relative success or difficulty in coping with it, with the mother's feelings about it, and her role in supporting it, and, not least, with the many ways teachers facilitate mastery (A. Freud, 1963, 1965; R. A. Furman, 1966; Archer and Hosley, 1969; E. Furman, 1969b, 1982, 1986; Daunton, 1990). We hoped that this knowledge and experience would enable us to be especially alert to and understanding of the toddlers' and mothers' ways of dealing with entry to nursery school, as well as assist us in observing the many new and different aspects we would inevitably encounter with these children and mothers.

Our most striking difference was that the Toddler Group youngsters had been observed, evaluated, and worked with intensively for one to two years, and even before that period, half of them had been known to their respective therapists since birth, and several since later infancy. These contacts had been part of the work around an older sibling's troubles who attended our Nursery School or Kindergarten, and had not been initiated because of concerns about the infant. Thus, at their time of entry into Nursery School, we already had long-term and in-depth understanding of their functioning and family relationships, as well as much opportunity to assess both the children's and parents' ability to utilize help and to respond to maturational changes. With other children, by comparison, all this is known minimally, despite our careful and detailed intake procedure.

Another marked difference was that the ex-toddlers' functioning was a good deal healthier and less encumbered by earlier conflicts than those youngsters who entered Nursery School without prior work in Toddler Group. In addition to phase-appropriate progress, they had essentially mastered bodily self-care, and achieved a considerable degree of impulse control and ability to tame their anger, had begun to engage in a true teacher–pupil relationship and cooperation with peers. They enjoyed a variety of activities and experienced pleasure in learning and achieving. Their fine progress and accomplishments were especially heartening to observe because a number of them had originally started Toddler Group with considerable difficulties, and it was surprising to note how well they had responded to the early intervention.

Also, the ex-toddlers were familiar with the setting, would use the same playground, and at times, even the same room they had used while in Toddler Group, and knew many of the staff. They knew what nursery school was about, and they and their mothers were well prepared.

All this applied to a much lesser extent to the Nursery School entrants who had not been in Toddler Group.

THE PREPARATORY PERIOD

Considering that the toddler "graduates" entering Nursery School were by that time largely healthier than our usual newcomers, had mastered many of the personality prerequisites to a much greater extent, and were much better prepared, was the developmental task of adjustment easier for them? In some respects the answer is "yes," in some "no," and in some respects it highlighted difficulties we had overlooked in other new entrants for a number of reasons. And since entry to Nursery School affects the mother as well as the child, and represents a developmental step in her relationship with her child, the relative pluses and minuses applied to mothers too.

All this had manifested itself already during the preparatory phase when the mothers and children were still in Toddler Group. The parents and children had Nursery School in mind long before we outlined our preparatory steps for them (chapter 2). The parents usually verbalized their concerns during the first parent–teacher conference at the end of February, subsuming them under the question, "Will he be ready?" With some youngsters or in some areas of functioning their question focused realistically on specific masteries and ways of furthering them. Even in these cases, however, the teachers were the ones to point out how well the child was progressing and how much they trusted that he would be "ready," while the mothers, not the fathers, voiced their misgivings. We soon learned that their real question was, "Will I be ready?" meaning, "I can't bear letting him grow up and away, although I so much want him to succeed at it."

The children showed their equally early thoughts about Nursery School by suddenly paying much more attention to it. Before that time even the toddlers who had siblings in the Nursery had ignored it. Now they lingered in the hallway to catch glimpses of the Nursery children and teachers, stopped to observe them when they met one, and commented that the Nursery children took the snack cart on their own whereas they wheeled it to and fro with mother and teacher. They looked into the Nursery School windows when we were on the playground, checked out which equipment they shared with the preschoolers, and which would become newly available to them, asked about the Nursery outside time, and watched the Nursery children coming out as we were ready to leave. They found our books about nursery school on the shelf, long before we had planned to read them, inquired about the kinds of puzzles the "bigger kids" use, noted that the cook was preparing lunch, and contemplated the idea of having lunch at school themselves one day. Although the toddlers' mixed feelings were evident throughout, they seemed to view themselves as preschoolers-to-be and focused on the task of learning about the new setting, and integrating it by pinpointing the similarities and differences between Toddler Group and Nursery School.

As the time grew closer, with scheduled visits by each Nursery teacher in the Toddler Group, with the mothers visiting the Nursery first on their own and then with their child, and with many discussions about the coming change, the children's and mothers' feelings surfaced much more prominently, sometimes in words and sometimes indirectly, in restlessness or a heightened pitch to their voices. We became quite alert to these signs, linked them with the immediate stimulus, and facilitated talking about them. A little hubbub on the day of the Nursery Teachers' visits signaled everyone's worry about them. Lots of noisy comments or hushed silence when reading the book about Nursery activities signaled the concern over the obvious absence of the mothers in the pictures and overrode the pleasure of noting the familiarity of the activities. The children's phase-appropriate concerns focused on: "How will I show up and, especially, how will I show up without my mother?" This was a question of comparative adequacy which was barely mitigated by assurance that mother would stay with them until they felt quite comfortable. Their own harsh consciences prompted many to worry that the future teachers might be very strict, even punitive, and set standards of impulse control and skill achievement which they, the children, would not be able to meet. After a Nursery teacher's visit these youngsters always commented how "nice" she was, that is, different from the image their conscience had formed. And there were some who anticipated mother's leaving as their main concern and even planned defensively not to need her or to start staying for lunch right away.

In all, these worries, in open and disguised form, were readily helped by individual and group discussions and, through their work with the therapists, the mothers participated well and also assisted their children at home. These were, after all, the familiar concerns which we always hope children will be able to voice and mothers will be able to hear, when we work with parents of new entrants. We know how difficult it is to achieve this kind of preparation when mothers and children are not yet in tune with one another, when both hope that stressing the positives will sweep the worries away. And we were also glad that the children's appropriate focus on anticipating the future left room for feelings about leaving Toddler Group. They kept close track of just how many days were left (at their request we also made a paperchain with six links, one for each child to remove during the last six classes). They thought about how they would keep us in mind during the vacation with toddler songs, activities, and letters, how they would visit us and we them after they started Nursery School. They proudly thought back over how far they had progressed, comparing their earlier and recent skills in doing puzzles, in painting pictures, in caring for themselves. There were thoughts about new toddlers who might get their cubbies and their teachers, there were some denigrations of Toddler Group to ease the pain of loss (you wouldn't miss something you don't like), there were some troubles in actually saying goodbye at the end.

On the whole, however, these concerns were minor compared to their wish and ability to forge ahead and to integrate the past, along with its losses, to better face the future. It was a striking contrast to the beginning of the Toddler Group period when even the end of class time, not to mention holiday breaks, were perceived as being "kicked out," and when so many thought that leavings could result only from anger or retribution for anger.

At the end of Toddler Group, it was the mothers who felt "kicked out." Many verbalized their sadness and reluctance to leave. Many cried during the last parent–teacher conference, and at the end of the last class. Many half-jokingly begged to be allowed to return to Toddler Group after their children settled in Nursery School, either just for the pleasure of doing it all over again or offering to assist us, or they were eagerly thinking ahead of enrolling a younger child. Some had difficulty scheduling their visits to the Nursery, mixed up dates or times, or simply forgot to keep their appointment. One toddler put it to his Mom like this: "Don't you want me to go there?" The differences between the children's and mothers' feelings were so marked that a number of mothers had to acknowledge and clarify them and assure their toddlers that they were also happy with their growing up, and would truly support them in becoming fine preschoolers. Needless to say, the teachers and therapists did their best to assist the mothers with their mixed feelings.

The mothers' feelings of loss and their hardship in anticipating the child's entry to Nursery School as a major change in the relationship do not usually enter the preparatory work with the parents of new entrants in our own or other preschools. In part this is due to these feelings being overshadowed by the mother's worry about how she will show up as a mother when exposing her child to the possibly critical view of outsiders. This worry tends to be so great, consciously or unconsciously, that mothers stake everything on having the child make a good impression and on conforming to the teachers' stated or perceived expectations. This is often carried to the point where they absent themselves as much as possible and hope thereby to prevent the child from having or showing trouble with separation feelings. When these defensive maneuvers are interfered with, as they are in our Nursery where the mothers have to participate in a lengthy adjustment period, their own feeling of loss usually overtakes them later when they start to worry less about showing up well and find themselves in the painful position of having to "be there to be left" (E. Furman, 1982). Toddler Group mothers worried much less about how they or their child would show up. They were also much more in touch with their maternal feelings. We hoped, therefore, that their preparatory awareness and work would help them. No doubt it did but, as we were to learn anew each year, preparation is not a substitute for the actual experience. It mitigates stress but does not prevent it.

We also wondered to what extent these mothers and/or their experiences in the Toddler Group were unusual and perhaps exacerbated their feelings. Careful comparison and sifting of data convinced us that the mothers were not unusual. The nature and intensity of their feelings about the developmental step of entry to nursery school was matched by the feelings of other mothers who experienced them without prior attendance in Toddler Group. Moreover, the toddlers' mothers had not been aware of their feelings until the work helped them to be more in tune with themselves and their child. A number of them had entered their older children in our Nursery and in other nurseries without anticipating their own feelings and with using multiple ways of warding them off. They had initially been similarly unaware of their feelings when, in Toddler Group, they struggled to maintain an infantile relationship with their child and could not view him as ready or eager to become a more independent toddler. Neither the mothers nor their feelings were unusual, only the ability to recognize and bear them.

The Toddler Group experience did, I think, add a special factor. First, it enabled the mothers to enjoy their toddlers, to enjoy feeling, thinking, and doing with them. Second, it often enabled them to recapture and reintegrate their own toddlerhood in a contained and supportive milieu. Both these aspects made the prospect of giving up this phase with their child more poignant. Other mothers often experience toddlerhood as so stressful and so devoid of gratification for themselves and their child that they hope to get it over with and look forward to the promised respite of the next phase. Little do they realize that it is far better to have had something and lost it, than never to have had it at all.

OLD AND NEW TROUBLES ON STARTING NURSERY SCHOOL

Our children had no difficulty in orienting themselves in the new setting of the Nursery, in knowing who their special teacher was, in learning the sequence of the activity periods, in taking care of their bodily needs, or in engaging skillfully in activities. In these respects they fared far better than most other newcomers. As their teachers put it: "They know what nursery school is all about"; and so did their mothers. It was all the more impressive to note how hard the children and mothers had to work at building the relationship with the new teacher, at gradually separating from each other, and, not least, at integrating the past Toddler Group experiences and ties into their current lives. At first we thought the adjustment was really harder for them, but then we realized that our close knowledge of them as well as their own and their mothers' ability to feel and to verbalize feelings, underscored the enormity of this developmental task and enabled us to appreciate it to an extent and in ways which had not been possible before. With other children and mothers, the difficulties in mastering the new environment, the bodily care, and their mutual mixed feelings tended to loom so large, the feelings were often so hard to reach, and our limited knowledge of them made us miss so many of the subtler behavioral clues. As a result, and despite our many years of experience and understanding, we had underestimated other aspects of the task.

The ex-toddlers' struggles to cope with the changes and new challenges did not manifest themselves loudly. There were no overwhelming anxiety tantrums, no major regressions in self-care, no marked losses of impulse control, no clinging, tearful, or aggressive separation problems. Rather, their stress and conflicts showed subtly, so subtly that they might have easily been missed or much minimized without the close observation in the classroom and the ongoing treatment-via-the-parents. Each child's and mother's way of coping were, of course, individual and utilized both current and earlier means. This reemergence of past responses, many of which had not been in evidence for months, was in itself a sign of the degree of difficulty. For example, some children's primitive mouth urges were brought back in the form of stuffing food or refusing it, of staring at the teacher or averting their eyes when near her, of "accidentally" getting playdough or paint in their mouths, or not "taking in" when called by name. Some mothers reverted to being intrusive, taking over their child's activities and feelings. They might be unable to let him think for himself as he began the day by, say, constructing a block building and misperceiving his disgruntled attitude to this activity as distress at mother's anticipated leaving. Some children sidestepped the relationship with the teacher by not showing her their good work or not asking for help with an unfamiliar task. They called her "teacher" instead of using her name. They would not share home experiences and did not want mother to tell about them either. At the same time, their mixed feelings about mother showed in involving her too much or not at all when she was in the classroom, visiting her too much or not at all when she was in the waiting room, having more trouble with getting ready to come to school or more trouble getting ready to leave school. The mothers, for their part, found it difficult to be appropriately available. At times they were there bodily but not emotionally, at times they forgot the agreed upon steps in the separation schedule and returned too early or too late, or failed to let the child and teacher know that they had returned. Some felt that the teacher was not sufficiently available to their child or to them, and others formed a close twosome with their child, distanced themselves from the teacher, and could not help the child to relate to her. Several mother–child couples found it as hard to give up the gratifications of playing and doing activities together as they had earlier found it hard to relinquish the shared bodily care.

The mothers and children who experienced most difficulty were those where the mothers had succeeded least in changing their relationship with the child in the direction of caring about him as a separate person. Not only was it harder for them to support and enjoy the child's steps toward greater independence, but they were more apt to respond to the perceived loss by leaving him first or by disinvesting him—not keeping him and his emotional needs in mind. This resulted in such incidents as a mother suddenly arranging a brief out-of-town trip for herself, or going out at night without letting her child know beforehand (so he woke and found himself alone with the sitter), or making weekend plans which excluded the child, or deciding to give away a pet. In each instance the distress related not just to the act itself but to the accompanying feeling or lack of feeling which emerged through the work. The children, of course, felt and reacted to their mothers' revived and heightened difficulty. It increased their anger and concern, made them engage mother more closely, "forget" about her, and/or disinvest themselves, perhaps by appearing absentminded. It also brought to the fore some related earlier or partly persisting home problems. For example, where mother's periodic disinvestment of her children had led to lack of supervision or protectiveness, siblings had often become overly aggressive and excited with each other, or the child had been left to play on his own and come to harm with household equipment, or was victimized by others in play groups or day care settings. As described earlier, the parents' complaints about their child's aggression with peers or his being mistreated by older siblings, though stated at referral to Toddler Group, were rarely observed in Toddler Group because mother was available and the treatment-via-the-parent work helped toward improvement at home. Nevertheless, these troubles resurfaced to an extent at entry to Nursery School, in part because of the mothers' increased difficulty and in part because now the children were in a setting in which they would be without mother's help. Thus, there were some minor incidents of children not being careful

of their safety, especially outdoors where everyone is more active, where teacher and child are often farther away from each
other, and some children therefore feel less protected. There
were also incidents of children being attracted to peers who
manifested excited–aggressive behavior and/or attempts to engage or provoke them to such interplays. Although these observations served to alert the youngsters and their mothers to the
difficulties and proved helpful in understanding them better,
the behaviors point up the increased stress.

Reviewing these experiences and discussing them repeatedly with our educational director, we learned anew just how
hard it is for mothers, children, and teachers to deal with the
many cross-currents of feelings which are an inevitable part
of integrating the new relationships with one another in their
threesome. We realized that even our Nursery teachers, with
their special awareness and feel for the mother–child relationship, focused much more on relating with the child and did not
sufficiently appreciate the extent of the mother–child dependence in this early preschool period. This intensified the mothers' left-out feelings and burdened the child in two main ways:
(1) by his inevitable response to mother's feelings, and (2) by
his not feeling fully accepted because mother is also a part of
him and when she is left out, a part of himself is left out. We
realized also that we encountered the same difficulty with other
newcomers but had been less aware of it just as they had been
less aware of it. The toddlers and their mothers, by contrast,
were especially aware of it because in the Toddler Group both
were accepted equally and the change was more marked for
them.

We shared our better understanding with the teachers and
mothers. Since they were familiar with our four steps toward
mastery of self-care, from doing for the child to his ultimately
doing for himself, we helped them view the process of learning
to go to school in these same terms. The Toddler Group is the
second step of "doing with the child" and entry to Nursery
School is the third step of "standing by to admire the child's
doing for himself." This is the step, or stage, which is always
the hardest for the mother because she feels not needed, although she is very much needed. At entry to Nursery School it

is the mother's task to begin to stand by to admire her child as he works at functioning on his own. It is the teacher's task to appreciate that mother and child have been in the "doing with the child" stage, to accept them as such, and to assist them empathically in making the transition to the next stage. Hard though this stage is, it will, and really did, lead to the desired last stage of enabling the child to internalize mother's loving support and to function comfortably in an independent way. This effort at clarifying matters for the mothers and teachers in familiar terms, and working with both to implement them in their daily interactions, proved very helpful. It did not eradicate the hardship but greatly increased their mutual understanding and acceptance and enabled them better to work together on behalf of the child.

INTEGRATING PAST AND PRESENT

In the Toddler Group we had learned that, sooner or later, each child brought up his prior experience with other children. It was only when we, the mothers and teachers, could appreciate it, compare it with the present setting, and empathize with their feelings, that they began to be really comfortable in the Toddler Group. Often even the mothers had not known what had transpired elsewhere or had not thought that it related to the Toddler Group. Often the specific experiences had been unhappy and were still troubling, such as a child having "pushed down the babies at the sitter's" or having been hurt by peers, not having had his mother with him, having observed sexual differences while others were being diapered, having been sent home for being "mean." Increasingly we realized, however, that happy memories needed to be shared and accepted in equal measure and that the children were particularly pleased when we did something very similar or even identical. There were songs they had also learned elsewhere, a puzzle they knew, a way of rolling out the playdough, or a familiar snack. In short, finding the similarities and differences between present and past was an important way of integrating the Toddler Group experience, and the adults' knowledge and acceptance of the facts and related feelings was an important part of the process. Sometimes the memories stemmed from play-grounds or day care, sometimes from experiences with siblings or relatives, sometimes mother had been with the child and sometimes not. We had always been very aware of a child's need to integrate home and school; for example, taking things from home to school and vice versa, comparing and accepting the different home and school rules as well as customs, such as different ways of serving food or of celebrating birthdays or of being allowed to use paints at school but not at home. But we had not paid so much attention to the need to integrate past with present group, school, or peer experiences.

When the toddlers entered Nursery School, this aspect of their adjustment process became very evident. They sang the songs they had learned in Toddler Group, used the outdoor equipment they had enjoyed there, talked about the plants they had grown there and were often still treasuring at home. Inso-far as the Nursery teachers could understand and feel with these memories, they served as a means of building the new teacher–pupil relationships. It was at first harder for the teach-ers to recognize those memories which showed in upset or mis-behavior; for example, the sadness, angry protest, or refusal to participate during stories which were read in the room where the Toddler Group meets, or the disobedience, misbehavior, or desolate wandering around in the playground where the Nursery teachers did not sit with them on the seesaw or accom-pany it with singing "Seesaw, Marjorie Daw." The intensity of feeling was often observed by the way they checked the still empty Toddler Group room on arrival from the hallway and, of course, by the way they greeted the toddler teachers when we visited in the Nursery School. These welcomes ranged from sobbing embraces and yells of "My Mrs. Furman" to shy waves or pained turning away. Most prominent, however, was the children's need to tell us about everything they were doing in Nursery School, how they were doing it, and which new things they had learned, "Now I can paint a house"; "See, I learned to do my zipper, watch!"; "Here we get the snack cart by our-selves. Will you watch me when it's my turn?" It became very clear that the youngsters were not only missing Toddler Group but were trying very hard to share with their old and new teachers their attempts at linking Toddler Group and Nursery School, that this was an important part of making the transition.

This was equally important for the mothers, though with them the sadness about the loss was initially greater as they stopped the toddler teachers wherever they saw us to reminisce about "good old times," to get sympathy for their loneliness, and support for their difficult task. Many were aware of their anger at us and at the change, but could also appreciate that they and their children would have had reason to be even more angry if we had tried to keep them in Toddler Group and had not recognized their being ready and able to go on. Only gradually did they begin to share with pleasure the new steps they and their children were taking: "Big week! Jeremy is ready to start having lunch at school"; "Ellen is doing very well. She even puts on her boots now."

Neither the mothers nor the children relinquished their ties to the Toddler Group and its teachers during the later years, but after the months of Nursery School adjustment were completed, the intensity of the feelings lessened, and so did the need to have us share in their progress. In time, with their mothers' support, the children came to view Toddler Group the way kind older brothers and sisters look at a younger one in the family, noticing and showing sympathetic interest in the new toddlers, inquiring about their activities, enjoying seeing or hearing about something they used to do. They even donated their outgrown tricycles or toys for the toddlers' use and sometimes brought in these items themselves, telling the awed little ones about having been in Toddler Group "a long time ago."

As soon as we came to appreciate better the role of integration in the transition, the Nursery teachers made a special effort to support it. They acquainted themselves more fully with the Toddler Group activities and songs, they solicited the children's comparisons ("How did you do it in Toddler Group?"; "Did you use the same cookie shapes? How were they different?"). They were alert to all the indirect signs of comparison and missing; for example, they prepared the children for using the "middle" room (i.e., the toddler room) for stories and talked with them about the related feelings; they picked up on memories or comments, and helped them write letters to the old teachers. Fortunately, one of the Nursery teachers shared my hobby of gardening and this became a much loved, continued interest and link.

Assisting the former toddlers with this kind of integration proved most helpful for them and their mothers. It considerably diminished the stress of the change, and greatly facilitated the building of the new relationships. It helped us also to reach out in a similar way to the new preschoolers who had not attended Toddler Group, who had been less able to bring their efforts at integration, and to have them understood. Yet they were in even greater need of empathy and support because they did not even have another child to share their past with, whereas the former toddlers often joined together and reminisced with one another. Indeed, some of the youngsters who had not been in Toddler Group envied the special relationship with the Toddler Group teachers. Sometimes their old teachers have come to visit and, of course, we always address their feelings and help to mitigate them, but it remains true and at times hard that the former toddlers have a bit of an advantage in opportunities for this kind of continuity and integration.

References

Archer, L., & Hosley, E. (1969), Educational program. In: *The Therapeutic Nursery School*, ed. R. A. Furman & A. Katan. New York: International Universities Press, pp. 21–63.

Daunton, E. (1990), The teachers' contribution to the therapeutic work at the Hanna Perkins School. Presented at the Forum of the Cleveland Center for Research in Child Development, April. *Child Anal.*, 3:37–57, 1992.

Freud, A. (1963), The concept of developmental lines. *The Psychoanalytic Study of the Child*, 18:245–265. New York: International Universities Press.

——— (1965), *Normality and Pathology in Childhood*. New York: International Universities Press.

Furman, E. (1957), Treatment of under-fives by way of parents. *The Psychoanalytic Study of the Child*, 12:250–262. New York: International Universities Press.

——— (1969a), Treatment via the mother. In: *The Therapeutic Nursery School*, ed. R. A. Furman & A. Katan. New York: International Universities Press, pp. 64–116.

——— (1969b), Observations on entry to nursery school. *Bull. Phila. Assn. Psychoanal.*, 19/3:133–152.

——— (1969c), Some thoughts on the pleasure in working. *Bull. Phila. Assn. Psychoanal.*, 19/4:197–212.

——— (1974), *A Child's Parent Dies*. New Haven, CT: Yale University Press.

——— (1980), Filial therapy. In: *Basic Handbook of Child Psychiatry*, ed.-in-chief J. D. Noshpitz, Vol. 3, *Therapeutic Interventions*, ed. S. I. Harrison. New York: Basic Books, pp. 149–158.

——— (1982), Mothers have to be there to be left. *The Psychoanalytic Study of the Child*, 37:15–28. New Haven, CT: Yale University Press.

——— (1984), Mothers, toddlers and care. In: *The Course of Life*, Vol. 2, *Early Childhood*, ed. S. I. Greenspan & G. H. Pollock. Madison, CT: International Universities Press, 1989, pp. 61–82.

——— (1985a), Play and work in early childhood. *Child Anal.*, 1:60–76, 1990.

——— (1985b), On fusion, integration and feeling good. *The Psychoanalytic Study of the Child*, 40:81–110. New Haven, CT: Yale University Press.

—— (1986), The roles of parents and teachers in the life of the young child. In: *What Nursery School Teachers Ask Us About: Psychoanalytic Consultations in Preschools,* ed. E. Furman. Madison, CT: International Universities Press, pp. 3–19.

—— (1987), *Helping Young Children Grow.* Madison, CT: International Universities Press.

—— (1990), Plant a potato: Learn about life (and death). *Young Children,* 46/1:15–20.

—— (1991), On feeling and being felt with. *The Psychoanalytic Study of the Child,* 47:67–84. New Haven, CT: Yale University Press, 1992.

—— (1992), *Toddlers and Their Mothers.* Madison, CT: International Universities Press.

—— Furman, R. A. (1989), Some effects of the one-parent family on personality development. In: *The Problem of Loss and Mourning: Psychoanalytic Perspectives,* ed. D. R. Dietrich & P. C. Shabad. Madison, CT: International Universities Press, pp. 129–157.

Furman, R. A. (1966), On separation at entry to nursery school. In: *What Nursery School Teachers Ask Us About: Psychoanalytic Consultations in Preschools,* ed. E. Furman. Madison, CT: International Universities Press, 1986, pp. 35–52.

—— (1983), The father-child relationship. In: *What Nursery School Teachers Ask Us About: Psychoanalytic Consultations in Preschools,* ed. E. Furman. Madison, CT: International Universities Press, 1986, pp. 21–34.

—— (1984), On toilet mastery. *Child Anal.,* 2:98–110, 1991.

—— Katan, A. (1969), *The Therapeutic Nursery School.* New York: International Universities Press.

Goldsborough, J. (1981), *I Can Do It By Myself.* New York: Golden Press.

Hägglund, T.-B. (1987), Discussion of R. A. Furman's "Sexual Seduction in Childhood: Some Child Analytic Perspectives." Presented at the scientific meeting of the Oulu Psychotherapy Foundation, Oulu, Finland, September.

Krauss, R. (1945), *The Carrot Seed.* New York: Harper & Brothers.

Leach, P. (1989), *Your Baby and Child.* New York: Knopf.

Seymour, D. Z. (1965), *Big Beds and Little Beds,* illustrated by G. Wiggins. New York: Wonder Books/Grosset & Dunlap.

Smith, E. G. (1957), *The Absolutely Perfect Book of Baby and Child Care.* New York: Harcourt, Brace.

Winnicott, D. W. (1953), Transitional objects and transitional phenomena. In: *Playing and Reality.* New York: Basic Books, 1971, pp. 1–25.

Name Index

Subject Index

Activities: goal as, in Toddler Group, 14–15; impulses and, 91–92, 95, 100, 102, 133, *see also* Impulses; integration of, in educational program, 38–40, 194–198, *see also* Educational program; mastery of, 32–40, 46, *see also* Mastery; materials selected, 24, 36–39; mother's role with, 39, 65, 217, *see also* Mother; Mother-toddler groups; peers, shared with, 205; play v. 178–179; pleasure in, 175, 210, *see also* Pleasure; sequence of, 9–11; specific, *see* Books; Gardening; Insects; Life-Cycle; Natural Environment; Plants; Self-care; teacher's role with, 14–15, 33, 189, *see also* Educational program; Interests; Learning; Learning-Teaching; Teacher-child relationship; Toddler teacher

Adoptive mother: 52

Aggression: *see* Impulses, aggressive

Anal impulses: *see* Impulses, excretory

Analysis: *see* Psychoanalysis

Anger: *see* Impulses, aggressive

Assessment:42–46, 209–211, 216–220, *see also* Follow-up; Nursery School, entry to; Parent-teacher conferences

Baby: father and, 52, 69–70; impulses of, 85, 90; mother and, 52–53, 90; self-investment, 53; sensations bodily, 139, *see also* Impulses, mouth; Investment, maternal; Mother; Mother-child relationship; Need satisfaction; Nursing; Sensations, bodily

Bathroom arrangements:7, 24; *see also* Hanna Perkins Mother-Toddler Group; Self-care; Privacy; Toileting

Bereavement:163–164, 196; *see also* Life-cycle; Separation

Big orange chairs: *see* Hanna Perkins Mother-Toddler Group

Birthday:22, 149, 207; *see also* Educational program; Self-care/Eating

Blankie: *see* Transitional object

Bodily care: *see* Investment, maternal; Mother; Mother-child relationship; Self-care

Bodily differences: *see* Differences, bodily

Bodily discharge: *see* Sensations, bodily

Bodily self: *see* Toddler/Self, concept of

Bodily self-care: *see* Self-care

Books:25, 39, 46, 189–191, *see also* Ac-